ting into

aw

Getting Into guides

Getting into

Law

Lianne Carter

9th edition

Getting into Law

This ninth edition published in 2012 by Trotman Publishing, an imprint of Crimson Publishing Ltd., Westminster House, Kew Road, Richmond, Surrey TW9 2ND.

Author: Lianne Carter

© Trotman Publishing 2008, 2010, 2012

© Trotman & Co Ltd 1994, 1996, 1999, 2002, 2004, 2006

British Library Cataloguing in Publication Data
A catalogue record for this book is available from the British Library.

ISBN 978 1 84455 481 2

Typeset by IDSUK (DataConnection) Ltd
Printed and bound by Ashford Colour Press, Gosport, Hants

Contents

Contents

Preface

Over the past few years the number of applicants for law courses has increased enormously. Furthermore, competition for places on what might be regarded as the 'best' university courses has become more intense as students are becoming increasingly aware that employers are looking carefully at which universities their prospective employees have attended.

During the course of MPW's work advising students on their choice of university course, we have gathered together a huge amount of information on law courses and the legal profession. With the encouragement of Trotman Publishing, that information has been brought together in this guide.

This edition has been substantially updated and revised with input from a number of people from the BPP Law Schools in London, Manchester and Leeds, and we are very grateful for their help. We would also like to thank the Law Society, the Bar Council, and UCAS. We hope that this guide will be of use to anyone considering law as a career.

MPW
November 2011

About the author

Lianne Carter studied Law LLB at Sussex University, graduating with first-class honours. She then worked as a legal consultant for Lawspeed Limited, advising clients on employment law and undertaking extensive legal research. Having decided that teaching was her vocation, Lianne now teaches Law A level at MPW's London college. Lianne would like to thank James Barton for his invaluable help and guidance when updating this book.

Acknowledgements

This edition of *Getting into Law* has been revised and updated by the following.

BPP contributors

Professor Peter Crisp
Dean of BPP Law School, London
After completing the Graduate Diploma in Law and the Bar Vocational Course, Peter practised in general Chancery work in Lincoln's Inn, specialising in property work of all kinds.

Mandy Gill
Managing Director of BPP's Law School in Manchester
Mandy qualified as a solicitor in 1993 and has been involved in vocational legal education since 1994.

Jonathan Haines
Managing Director of BPP's Law School in Leeds
A City-trained solicitor with international firm Allen & Overy, Jonathan has an LLM from London University and is currently a member of the Legal Practice Course board, which oversees the Legal Practice Course.

Jill Livingstone
Lecturer in Business Law and Practice at BPP's Law School in Manchester
Jill qualified as a solicitor in 1997 and spent seven years in the corporate department of Eversheds LLP before joining BPP in April 2005.

Professor Carl Lygo
Principal, BPP Law Schools in Leeds, London and Manchester
Carl read law at university and has a research master's degree in law. He qualified as a barrister and practised in Leeds and London. Carl has taught at Leeds University, City University London and the University of East Anglia.

Other contributors

Rahim Shamji
Rahim Shamji is a lecturer in criminal litigation, evidence and advocacy. He is a practising member of the bar at Mitre House Chambers, London, and a Qualified Mediator from the International Mediation Training Programme. His areas of practice are crime and human rights.

Abigail Flack

Abigail Flack is a qualified lawyer. She specialised in corporate transactions and is now a lecturer in business law and practice and equity finance at BPP Law School, London.

Nicola Zoumidou

Nicola Zoumidou studied law at the Universities of Bristol and Fribourg (in Switzerland). After graduation, Nicola worked at an international law firm in Paris before completing her LPC in London and then trained and qualified as a solicitor at a small commercial firm in the City of London. She then moved to a national firm of solicitors in the UK before deciding to join BPP. She completed the STEP qualification whilst in practice and served on the Law Society's Probate Section Executive Committee from 2004 to 2007. Nicola now teaches on the Legal Practice Course at Manchester Law School.

Neil Stewart

Neil Stewart is manager of BPP College's Waterloo library. He holds master's degrees from the University of Manchester in International Relations, and from University College, London in Library and Information Studies. He is a member of the British and Irish Association of Law Librarians.

James Burnett

James Burnett is a Director of Studies and careers advisor at Mander Portman Woodward. He is the author of a number of the books in this series, including Getting into Business, Economics and Management Courses.

Thanks are also due to the contributors to the earlier editions of the book, in particular Fiona Hindle, Dr James Holland, Julian Webb, Paul Whiteside, Mike Semple Piggot, Frances Burton, Joanne Hubert and Justina Burnett.

Introduction

Unless this book has just slipped off the shelf into your hands and fallen open at this very page, you're probably reading it hoping to pick up some pearls of wisdom on whether or not you should study law. This guide is intended to answer those questions you've always wanted to ask and possibly a few more that have never crossed your mind.

This book will start with an introduction to the legal profession, an overview of the UK's legal systems, and a discussion of what lawyers do and how they fit into the legal system.

The next few chapters will then run through how a person goes about qualifying as a lawyer, including the different qualification routes, and the importance of work experience.

The rest of the chapters deal with everything you need to know about the university application process, including choosing the right university law course, what to do on results day, and an overview of the new arrangements for fees and funding.

At the end of the book there is a useful glossary of terms, both legal and university-application related.

Don't be fooled, however, into thinking that *Getting into Law* will do all the work for you so you can put your feet up and watch *Law and Order* on TV!

You will still have to . . .

- revise thoroughly and pass your exams. You can get on to a few university courses with fairly low grades, but those courses might not suit your needs. You'd be better off with higher grades and a wider choice of degree options available to you.

You should also . . .

- be a legal eagle. Do your own research. Talk to your teachers, friends, family, legal practitioners, anyone who might know something about the legal profession. Consider carefully what type of course is appropriate for you. Or, come to that, whether you should even think about studying law in the first place. Remember the law of the jungle. It is a competitive world out there!

1 | An introduction to the legal profession

Most people's first impressions of the legal profession come from the glamorous world of film or television. Programmes such as *Law and Order*, *Silk*, *Franklin and Bash*, and even *Legally Blonde* paint a picture of lawyers striding heroically across the courtroom of life standing up for truth and justice. But what are lawyers and what do they actually do?

The term 'lawyer' is a loose one that covers barristers, solicitors, judges, in-house legal advisors, paralegals, legal executives, some civil servants and academic lawyers. In England and Wales (the legal systems of Scotland and Northern Ireland are discussed later on in the book), the crucial distinction to make is between the two main branches of the profession: solicitors and barristers. The essential difference between them relates to their respective rights to advocate on behalf of a client in court: traditionally only barristers were permitted to undertake advocacy on behalf of a client in the highest courts. This distinction means that law is sometimes referred to as a 'split' profession – but in fact the split is increasingly becoming blurred due to modern reforms that permit solicitors to undertake further training and then represent clients in the higher courts. More information on this is given in the paragraphs below. (The term 'attorney' is American and has no real meaning in the UK.)

> **Solicitors** work on all aspects of the law, but do not normally present their clients' cases in court.
>
> **Barristers** are instructed by solicitors to represent their clients in the courtroom.

Solicitors

Solicitors are often described as being like medical general practitioners (GPs). They deal directly with their clients and often have an ongoing professional and/or business relationship with them. Solicitors in private practice group together in law firm partnerships, with the senior solicitors being partners and the more junior solicitors being employed associates. Solicitors may deal with different aspects of the law, although increasingly they deal with specific areas, for example employment or family law or, in the City, with specialist areas such as syndicated loans, bonds or takeovers and mergers. Generally speaking, law firms cover a wide area of legal practice; this means that in smaller firms lawyers may be required to cover a broad range of areas, whereas the larger law firms will have specialists in very narrow areas of law.

Historically, solicitors could only appear in lower courts, such as the magistrates' and county courts. These days, however, solicitors who obtain higher rights of audience can now appear in the Supreme Court and may even apply to become a QC (Queen's Counsel), although this is still rare.

The Law Society is the body which represents solicitors in England and Wales. The Law Society Regulation Board used to be responsible for the regulation of solicitors, but in January 2007 the Solicitors Regulation Authority was established to deal with all regulatory and disciplinary matters, including:

- administering the role of solicitors
- drafting the rules of professional conduct
- setting qualification standards.

Barristers

Barristers have traditionally been described as more like medical consultants. They are 'self-employed referral professionals' who are often, although not exclusively, trial lawyers – meaning that they appear robed and wigged in court on behalf of their clients. Clients are usually referred to them by a professional advisor, often a solicitor – although reforms introduced in 2004 allow barristers to see the public directly where the Bar Council has agreed that no referral is necessary (for example in relation to tax advice when referred by an accountant).

It is usual for barristers (often called counsel) to specialise in certain areas of law, for example common law, criminal law, company law or tax law and so on. Barristers in private practice group together in chambers, sharing overheads and office support, but remaining self-employed professionals.

Barristers are governed by the General Council of the Bar (known as the Bar Council). The Bar Council's main role is to represent barristers, and in 2006 the regulatory role was delegated to the Bar Standards Board. Similar to the Solicitors Regulation Authority, the Bar Standards Board's functions include setting education and training requirements for barristers, setting the standards of conduct for barristers, and taking disciplinary action where necessary.

Size and make-up of the legal profession (England and Wales)

The solicitors' profession in England and Wales is the largest branch of the legal profession. In 2010 its governing body, the Law Society (www.lawsociety.org.uk), reported that there were 150,128 registered solicitors and 117,862 of these held a practising certificate. To qualify as a solicitor you would normally be expected to complete a training contract period of employment that lasts two years. In the year to July 2010 the Law Society reported that 4,874 new training contracts were registered.

In 2010 the average age of a male solicitor was 44.4 and the average age of a female solicitor was 38.1, which illustrates how rapidly the profession has grown in the last 15–20 years. The solicitors' profession is divided between solicitors who work in private practice for law firms and those who work 'in-house' (i.e. for companies, government legal departments and so on). In 2010 there were 10,413 private law firms employing 86,748 solicitors, with just over 42% of these firms based in the south-east of England employing 53% of all solicitors. Solicitors employed outside private practice amounted to around 31,000.

The barristers' profession, known as the Bar, is much smaller than the solicitors' profession. According to the Bar Council (www.barcouncil.org.uk), in December 2010 there were a total of 15,387 barristers at the practising Bar. This is made up of 12,420 self-employed barristers of whom 32% were women and 7% described themselves as belonging to an ethnic minority. A further 2,967 barristers are in employed practice of whom 46% are female and 12% described themselves as belonging to an ethnic minority.

In 2010, whilst 1,742 were 'called to the Bar' (see Chapter 4 for more information on this), only 460 obtained pupillage (the mandatory 12-month training stage for those who want to practise as a barrister).

Do I need a law degree?

The legal profession in England and Wales is virtually unique in not requiring all entrants to have a law degree. In fact, in September 2008 3,878 non-law graduates embarked upon the full-time Graduate Diploma in Law programme (an intensive one-year conversion course for non-law graduates covering the essential foundations taught on a three-year law degree). Law firms and barristers' chambers typically claim to recruit around 40% of their intake from non-law graduates.

According to the Higher Education Statistics Agency (www.hesa.ac.uk), about 16,250 students obtained undergraduate law degrees in 2010.

This number continues to rise each year: 14,655 students had obtained undergraduate law degrees in 2006 and 12,635 students had obtained undergraduate law degrees in 2004. However, the limited number of places available on postgraduate law courses means that many undergraduate law students do not carry on to qualify as solicitors or barristers. At the start of the 2009–10 academic year, 7,064 students from all backgrounds began vocational training as a solicitor (the Legal Practice Course) and 1,793 students began vocational training as a barrister (the Bar Vocational Course).

The other thing to be aware of is that not every law degree is recognised by the professional bodies as a qualifying law degree (QLD) – it all depends on the subjects that are studied on the course. This means that you must be careful when choosing your course: only a QLD will give exemption from the academic stage of training. The Law Society and the Bar Council keep records of which degrees are QLDs. See Chapter 6 for further details.

Women in the legal profession

It is difficult to imagine that less than 100 years ago the legal profession was the preserve of the male. Things have changed and are still changing. Law schools report that as many as two-thirds of all new students undertaking vocational legal training are female. About 46% of practising solicitors are female, and about 5.5% of solicitors are female partners. There is a feeling within the solicitors' profession that not enough female solicitors make it to partnership in some of the very large law firms.

About 33% of practising barristers are female, with 52% of new entrants undertaking pupillage being female. Whereas in the past it was difficult for females to break down the traditional barriers, today the profession is increasingly open to all. This is evident in the fact that in 2009–10 there were 100 more women called to the Bar than men. However, there is still plenty of progress to be made by women in terms of judicial appointments. Only one woman has made it to the most senior law lord appointment, whilst roughly 10% of high court and circuit judges are female. At the lower level, 25.6% of district judges and deputy district judges are female.

What if I don't want to go into the law after my degree?

Some students study law with no intention of becoming a professional lawyer. The legal knowledge and additional skills gained from a law degree are highly prized and can be applied to a number of jobs. We will look at those skills in more detail in Chapter 4.

But what else can a law graduate do other than law? If you use Clive Anderson, Bill Clinton or Tony Blair as your role models, the world is your oyster, but here are a few suggestions as to what the rest do.

- **Accountancy.** Many aspects of accountancy relate to those found in legal practice, such as analysing large amounts of technical material, analysing and writing reports and advising clients. Law graduates are often particularly attracted by tax consultancy. Starting salaries are usually high.
- **Administration.** You need a methodical and precise approach as well as good written and communication skills for this job. Some administrative work is in private industry but most jobs are found in the civil service, local government, the health service, voluntary organisations and further and higher education institutions.
- **Civil service.** Interested in policy making and implementation? Then you might think about civil service departments with legal responsibilities such as the Home Office, HM Revenue and Customs, Ministry of Justice, and Foreign and Commonwealth Office. Local authorities also value law graduates highly.
- **Business management.** The skills you develop from a law degree will be invaluable in the world of commerce and industry.
- **The City and finance.** A number of law graduates are lured into the highly paid world of investment banking and insurance where their legal background will give them an edge. But beware: competition is extremely tough for these high rewards.

In addition to the above areas, law graduates also go into legal publishing, the media, journalism (legal or otherwise), the police service, teaching, human resources and a lot more.

Some law graduates choose not to pursue the training to become either a solicitor or a barrister but would still like to do something legally related. They will often move into fields such as paralegal and clerking work. Paralegals research cases, scan and collate documents. Clerks undertake duties such as taking witness statements on behalf of solicitors' clients and conducting legal research for solicitors, barristers and others plus any administrative work that is required.

Case study

Karen did not consider a legal career until speaking to a careers advisor after her A level exams. She chose to study a law degree hoping it would open doors to whichever career she decided to pursue. Over the course of the degree she was fascinated by law as a subject and its relevance to everyday life. After her degree Karen decided to gain some commercial experience in the legal sector. She began training as a law costs draftsman; someone who deals with cases after they have concluded and draws up bills of the work done in order for the solicitor to be paid. The role of a law costs draftsman includes negotiating costs when they are disputed by paying parties, and attending hearings as an advocate to argue these costs. Karen enjoys the fact that legal costs is a fast-moving, exciting area of law, and believes that a career as a costs draftsman would be ideal for someone who is mathematically minded, yet also enjoys advocacy.

2 | The UK's legal systems

This chapter looks predominantly at the English legal system; however, key areas where Scottish and Northern Irish law differ are highlighted at the end of the chapter. Welsh law mainly follows that of England, but there are a few important differences, such as the Welsh Language Act 1993 which puts the Welsh language on equal footing with English in Wales. See www.assemblywales.org for more information.

The English legal system

English law comes from two main sources: statute law made by Parliament (also known as 'Acts of Parliament' or 'legislation') and case law made by judges (also known as 'common law'). The UK's membership of the European Union and the Human Rights Act 1998 have also significantly impacted on the English legal system. These sources will be summarised below, together with a brief description of the court structure.

Statute law

Parliament is the supreme law-making body in the English legal system, and is made up of the House of Commons, the House of Lords, and the Monarch. The House of Commons is made up of democratically elected Members of Parliament (MPs) from various political parties, and it is the political party that has the majority of MPs elected to the House of Commons that will form a government. (Note: in the 2010 election no political party gained a majority, which is why a coalition government was formed.)

The House of Lords is made up of the most senior bishops in the Church of England and peers who are nominated by the Prime Minister and then appointed by the Monarch. Since the 1990s, there have been calls for reform of the House of Lords, including the request that a proportion of the members be democratically elected. In May 2011 the government published draft legislation on reform of the House of Lords, which at the time of writing is being debated.

New laws are mostly put forward by the government, and the draft legislation has to go through several stages of debates and votes in both the House of Commons and the House of Lords. In the vast majority of cases, the draft legislation has to be approved by both Houses in order for it to become law. The final stage in the legislative process is Royal Assent, which is where the Monarch gives approval to the draft legislation and at this point it becomes an Act of Parliament. This is merely a formality, and the last time that a monarch refused assent was in 1707.

Acts of Parliament cannot be challenged by the courts, and can only be changed by a subsequent legislation. Acts of Parliament are also known as 'primary legislation' because they are made by Parliament, the supreme law-making body. Parliament can delegate its law-making power to other bodies, including government departments and local authorities, and law made by such bodies is known as delegated legislation or secondary legislation. Delegated legislation is subject to the control of Parliament and can be challenged in the courts.

Common law

Although Parliament is the supreme law-making body, and judges are simply supposed to apply the laws made by Parliament in cases, the doctrine of Judicial Precedent and the rules of Statutory Interpretation mean that in practice judges also make law through decided cases. This is known as 'case law' or 'common law' and is a major source of law in the English legal system.

The doctrine of Judicial Precedent is based on the Latin maxim *'stare decisis'* which means 'stand by what has been decided', so, very simply, when a judge makes a decision in a case, this should be followed in future cases that are similar. The system of precedent operates through the court hierarchy, so that only certain courts create binding precedents (precedents that must be followed in future cases). Precedents are created when a new situation or point of law comes up in a case that is not provided for in legislation and has not been decided in a previous case, so the judge has to decide the case by looking at situations that are similar and use reasoning by analogy.

When judges are applying legislation to cases before them, it is not always possible to simply take the words of the statute and decide the case, because words can have more than one meaning. In addition new technology and changes in society can mean that it is not clear whether the legislation applies in some cases. This is where the rules of statutory interpretation come in, and some judges take a 'literal approach' of applying the ordinary meaning of the words in the legislation even if this leads to an absurd result, whereas other judges take a 'purposive approach' and decide the case based on what they think Parliament wanted to achieve through the legislation. When a judge makes an interpretation in a case, this can create a precedent so that future cases must follow this interpretation.

Common law as a source of law only works because of the system of law reporting in England and Wales; an accurate record of decided cases is kept so that it can be referred to by judges and lawyers in future cases. It is mostly decisions of the higher courts in the English legal system that are reported, and all High Court, Court of Appeal and Supreme Court cases are now available on the internet, for example from www.bailii.org.uk.

The effect of European Union law

In 1973 the UK joined the European Economic Community (EEC), which was established in 1957 by Germany, France, Italy, Belgium, the Netherlands and Luxembourg. In 1993 the EEC became the European Union (EU). Over the years European law has had an increasing impact on the legal systems of Member States, and since 2007 there have been 27 Member States.

The European Union produces its own primary and secondary legislation, and has its own court, the European Court of Justice. Case law has confirmed that European law is supreme over the national laws of Member States, and that national law must be interpreted in accordance with European law.

The effect of the Human Rights Act 1998

The Human Rights Act 1998 officially incorporated the European Convention on Human Rights into the English legal system. The Convention sets out certain fundamental rights of the citizens of Europe, including the right to life, the right to a fair trial and the right to respect for private and family life. Prior to the Human Rights Act 1998, English citizens who believed that their Human Rights had been infringed had to take their case to the European Court of Human Rights in Strasbourg. The Human Rights Act 1998 means that such cases can now be dealt with in the courts of the English legal system.

The Human Rights Act 1998 has affected the English legal system in several other ways, including obligations that our courts must take into account any decision of the European Court of Human Rights, and, so far as is possible to do so, interpret national legislation so that it is compatible with the European Convention on Human Rights. All draft legislation must also state whether or not it is compatible with the Convention.

The court structure

The court structure in England is divided into two systems: those courts with civil jurisdiction and those with criminal jurisdiction. Civil cases are private disputes between individuals or companies, and there are many different types of civil law including family law, employment law, the law of contract, the law of tort and commercial law. Criminal cases are where the state prosecutes people for breaking laws, even though there is usually a victim.

Most civil cases are heard, in the first instance, by the County Court, but in cases where large amounts of money are in dispute, they will initially be heard in the High Court. Appeals from both the County Courts and the High Court can be made up through the court hierarchy.

All minor criminal matters are dealt with by the Magistrates' Court. Serious cases are referred to the Crown Court. Here, the case will be decided upon by a lay jury, a fundamental part of the Criminal Justice System. Cases can be appealed from the Magistrates' Court to the Crown Court and from there to the Court of Appeal (Criminal Division).

The highest court in the land, not only for England and Wales, but also for Scotland and Northern Ireland, is the new Supreme Court, formerly known as the House of Lords, which only considers appeals that concern points of law of general public importance. Each case is normally heard by five Justices of the Supreme Court. When a court is considering a point of European law it may refer to the European Court of Justice in Luxembourg for interpretation. The Judicial Committee of the Privy Council is the final Court of Appeal for the 24 Commonwealth territories and six independent republics within the Commonwealth. In 2004, the Privy Council heard 68 appeals. By far the most contentious work relates to appeals against the death penalty.

Judges

In contrast with those of many other European countries, the judiciary in England and Wales is not a separate career. Judges are appointed from both branches of the legal profession.

Judges in the Supreme Court are known as Justice of the Supreme Court (formerly Law Lords in the House of Lords), judges in the Court of Appeal are known as Lord Justices of Appeal, and judges in the High Court are known as High Court Judges.

Circuit Judges, Recorders and District Judges are the remaining three types of judges. Circuit Judges sit either in the Crown Court (to try criminal cases) or in the County Courts (to hear civil cases). Recorders are part-time judges who sit in the Crown Court, and District Judges sit in the Magistrates' Court and County Court.

Alternatively, a panel of lay magistrates can try criminal cases in the Magistrates' Court. They are not legally qualified or paid but are respected members of the community who sit as magistrates on a part-time basis.

All new members of the judiciary are now selected by the Judicial Appointments Commission, an independent body that was created specifically for this purpose following the Constitutional Reform Act

2005. Once appointed, judges are completely independent of both the legislature and the executive, and so are free to administer justice without fear of political interference.

Tribunals

A system of tribunals operates alongside the court system. Each type of tribunal specialises in certain types of cases. Almost all tribunals have been created by statute. For example, Employment Tribunals handle disputes and all aspects of work-related incidents. This includes disputed deductions from wages, unfair dismissal, redundancy and discrimination. An Employment Tribunal is a more informal setting than a court. There are no judges; tribunals are headed by a chairman who is appointed by the Lord Chancellor from a list of suitable applicants drawn up by the Independent Tribunal Service. In Employment Tribunals, for example, a chairman will be assisted by two lay members. There is no standard form of procedure. Nonetheless, they operate in a similar way to court proceedings, with witnesses usually giving evidence on oath.

Reform

The English legal system is constantly changing, so it is very important you keep up to date if you are thinking about a legal career. A good habit is to read the relevant press such as the legal pages of the major newspapers (e.g. *The Times*). Also look at professional journals such as *The Law Society Gazette* and *The Lawyer.*

The Scottish legal system

Scotland has its own legal system, with significant differences from those of the other constituent nations of the United Kingdom. The two fundamental differences are the role of the Scottish Parliament in formulating legislation, and the basis of Scottish jurisprudence in a mixed system of uncodified civil law and common law.

Since 1999, the Scottish Parliament has been responsible for legislating on a wide range of domestic matters relating to Scotland, but there are certain policy areas reserved for the UK Parliament at Westminster. Notably, these include constitutional matters, defence and national security policy, foreign policy, and fiscal and economic policy. Scotland's legal system and court structure is separate and autonomous from that of England and Wales, and Northern Ireland. Historically, it has its basis in Roman law, with some English common law influence since the Act of Union of 1707. Recent developments in Scottish law have seen the strong influence of English (and other jurisdictions') common law, as well as the influence and incorporation of European Union law.

While some areas of law are similar to that of England, Scotland has its own system of criminal law and procedure, of civil procedure, and of certain areas of private law. The court system reflects these differences, with its own system of separate criminal and civil courts. By way of illustration, Scottish criminal courts do not have the Supreme Court as the highest court of appeal, instead the Court of Session is Scotland's supreme court for civil cases, and the High Court of Justiciary is Scotland's supreme court for criminal cases. Most cases are either dealt with in the sheriff court, which deals with civil cases and more serious criminal offences, or the Justice of the Peace court, which deals with less serious criminal offences. The legal profession in Scotland will be discussed in Chapter 3.

> For more information see www.scotland.gov.uk/Topics/Justice/legal

The Northern Irish legal system

Like Scotland, Northern Ireland (NI) has a legal system separate from that of England and Wales. Unlike Scotland, NI's legal system to a large extent mirrors that of England and Wales, with the following differences.

In terms of legislative law, the Northern Ireland Assembly (which gained legislative powers in 1999) has the power to make laws for NI, with the proviso that Westminster-created laws still apply to NI. The Assembly can, however, modify Westminster's provisions in so far as they relate to NI. Westminster also reserves a number of areas of policy-making for itself, including foreign relations, nationality and immigration, and fiscal and economic policy.

NI has its own court system (the Northern Ireland Court Service), which parallels that of England and Wales. It includes the Court of Appeal, the High Court of Justice in Northern Ireland, and the Crown Court. The highest court of appeal for both criminal and civil matters, as in England and Wales, is the Supreme Court. Judicial law in NI is based on English common law and the doctrine of judicial precedent, and has developed on very similar lines to that of English common law. English precedent from the higher courts is not, however, binding, but is deemed to be persuasive. The higher Northern Irish courts also pay attention to important decisions made in the Republic of Ireland (ROI), the major Commonwealth nations and even the USA. The legal profession in Northern Ireland will be discussed in Chapter 3.

> For more information please see www.nidirect.gov.uk/justice and www.niassembly.gov.uk

3| What do lawyers do?

As discussed in Chapter 1, the legal profession in England and Wales is divided into two main branches: solicitors and barristers. This chapter will run through the working practices of each of the branches of the profession in more detail. At the end of the chapter there is an overview of the legal profession in Scotland and Northern Ireland.

Solicitors

As discussed in Chapter 1, about 74% of all practising solicitors work in private practice for law firms; the rest work either in-house for companies or for government agencies, etc. Solicitors' work is as diverse as life itself – they will be behind the scenes offering guidance to their clients on everything from train disasters to corporate takeovers. The working life varies enormously from firm to firm. For example, in a large firm it is not unusual to be engaged on one large case for several months, whereas in a small firm you may have 15 or more cases on the go at one time.

This section offers some examples of the work that solicitors undertake and an overview of the types of organisation that employ them.

Large corporate firms

The largest law firms by turnover tend to be law firms specialising in corporate law and are usually based in London. There is a 'Magic Circle' of elite national and international law firms with bases in London that rank as some of the largest law firms in the world. This analysis is done yearly and changes slightly based on the performance of the firms from year to year.

The latest commentary at the time of writing comes from *The Lawyer* (www.thelawyer.com) which states that the Magic Circle firms are:

- Clifford Chance LLP (3,385* lawyers)
- Freshfields Bruckhaus Deringer (2,634 lawyers)
- Linklaters LLP (2,597 lawyers).

* Note. These figures are liable to fluctuation in times of financial difficulty.

All figures for lawyers at law firms in this chapter relate to the number of world-wide fee earners and the figures are taken from *The Lawyer* at the date of writing. Recently the legal profession has seen the emergence of a number of firms which are not quite classed as Magic Circle, but are ranked above the 'Silver Circle' of law firms, which are the new elite firms challenging the Magic Circle law firms on profit and revenue per partner calculations. The quality of clients and lawyers, overall levels of revenue, and international scope in both work and presence are also taken into account.

Those firms almost within the Magic Circle and ranked above the Silver Circle are:

- Allen & Overy (2,543 lawyers)
- Herbert Smith LLP (1,410 lawyers)
- Ashurst (927 lawyers)
- Slaughter & May (748 lawyers).

The Silver Circle firms are:

- SJ Berwin LLP (625 lawyers)
- Macfarlanes (305 lawyers)
- Travers Smith (255 lawyers).

A recent trend has also developed for large US law firms to open branches in London, which contrasts with a less recent trend that has seen major London law firms expanding internationally.

The London branches of these US law firms are developing fast, and include:

- Skadden, Arps, Slate, Meagher & Flom LLP (1,923 lawyers)
- White & Case (1,894 lawyers)
- Latham & Watkins (1,595 lawyers)
- Weil, Gotshal & Manges (1,200 lawyers)
- Shearman & Sterling (963 lawyers).

In addition to the Magic Circle and Silver Circle, some other major international law firms are:

- DLA Piper (2,706 lawyers)
- Lovells LLP (1,785 lawyers)
- Norton Rose LLP (1,182 lawyers)
- CMS Cameron McKenna LLP (963 lawyers)
- Simmons & Simmons (939 lawyers)
- Denton Wilde Sapte LLP (752 lawyers)
- Clyde & Co. (702 lawyers).

Large law firms tend to offer a comprehensive service to corporate clients, covering areas such as:

- banking/finance law
- capital markets
- commercial litigation
- commercial property law
- company law
- competition law
- employment and pensions law
- financial regulatory law
- law relating to overseas jurisdictions
- mergers and acquisitions
- technology, media and telecommunications law.

Work is often undertaken by teams, with little or no direct contact with the client. A typical area of work for a trainee involves conducting practical legal research or undertaking document work known as 'due diligence'. Starting salaries for graduates can be as high as £30,000 with the possibility of earning £55,000 on qualification.

Large corporate law firms tend to demand extremely high standards from their lawyers, who are well known for working long hours. In exchange, however, these firms offer excellent training and it is not unusual for them to cater for your every need (gym in the basement, hairdresser, dry cleaner, shoe-shine service, beds in case you need to work through the night and need a quick snooze, somebody to get a present for your partner . . . all to avoid you having to leave your desk!).

Case study

Amrik Tumber qualified as a solicitor in 2005 at Sykes Anderson LLP, aged 26, and now works for Herbert Smith LLP in London.

'Before graduating with LLB Honours in Law at Staffordshire University, I was acutely aware of my desire to work for a London-based practice on corporate transactions. I acted on this awareness by applying for training contracts in the penultimate year of my degree. Ideally, I would have undertaken work experience in a City practice and obtained that coveted training contract soon thereafter, but that was not to be!

Instead, having graduated, I undertook my LPC at the College of Law and, after numerous applications and interviews, landed a training contract with Sykes Anderson (at the time, one of the smallest legal outfits in the City). Undoubtedly, I learned a great degree at Sykes Anderson, particularly regarding client, time and transaction management and not to mention early and challenging responsibility.

What Sykes Anderson could not meet however, largely due to its size, was my desire to work on large, complex and international corporate transactions. With this in mind, on qualification I made applications to the large players in the City and eventually landed a place as a corporate associate with Herbert Smith. The rest, as they say, is history!

Although there is no escaping the high professional standards and commitment that firms like Herbert Smith demand, I have a great set of work colleagues, the environment is congenial and importantly I feel good about my career and the work I do (well, mostly!).'

Major national law firms

If London is not for you, then there are some very large national law firms with a major presence in large cities such as Birmingham, Bristol, Leeds, Manchester and Newcastle. Some of these firms also have offices abroad, or have associate offices abroad. These major national law firms include:

- Eversheds (1,898 lawyers)
- Pinsent Masons (1,099 lawyers)
- Beachcroft Wansbroughs (978 lawyers)
- Irwin Mitchell (976 lawyers).
- Addleshaw Goddard (736 lawyers)
- Hammonds (622 lawyers)

Most of the larger law firms will sponsor students by paying their course fees for all postgraduate legal professional study and in many cases also offering a maintenance grant. Starting salaries for trainees tend to be high, with typical training contract salaries ranging from about £28,000 to £35,000 per annum and some firms offering at least £50,000 upon qualification. Usually the larger law firms recruit two to three years ahead of when they expect the trainee to start work, and most will have a vacation placement scheme which typically takes place twice yearly, during the Easter and summer periods. As you can imagine, the large law firms tend to be massively over-subscribed. It is not unusual for a lawyer to leave a large law firm once qualified and move to a smaller firm for what is regarded as a better quality of life (i.e. shorter working hours).

Case study

Jules Smith read for a BA in Communication Studies and Management at the University of Leeds and gained a 2:1 Honours degree. She is now a second-year trainee at Beachcroft LLP.

'After leaving university I actually began to carve out a career in journalism, but soon I realised that simply deconstructing press releases and rewriting them wasn't for me! I wanted to be able to use my brain in my work. I was first inspired to go into law when I realised how integrated with the functions of business the law really is. I am also very competitive!

I was delighted when I secured a training contact with Beachcroft LLP's Leeds office. They are one of the largest law firms nationally with prestigious offices in the big regional cities. They are a commercial practice and I joined them in September 2006. I have already completed seats [experience in different departments] in professional indemnity and construction and I am currently working in commercial property. When I qualify, I am hoping to focus mainly on litigation as, thankfully, I work best under pressure, and litigation is all about pressure.

I wanted to stay in the north after graduation. I studied in Leeds with BPP Law School so was pleased to be offered a training contract in the Leeds area. I was lucky to secure my training contract fairly early on and the firm helped me with my course fees. I immensely enjoyed my studies, and am sure I made the right choice!'

Smaller law firms

These make up the largest number of law firms, and range in size from one solicitor (sole practitioner) to firms with over 50 lawyers. They tend to specialise in areas more relevant to individuals than companies, or have smaller company clients. For example, on most high streets or in smaller town centres you will find at least one small firm dealing with:

- civil litigation (disputes between individuals)
- conveyancing (sale and purchase of property)
- criminal law
- employment law
- family law
- wills and trusts.

Due to the location of their offices, they tend to be categorised as high street firms – but remember that small firms can still offer high quality corporate work if they have the clients, and every high street is surrounded by small businesses! Do not forget that most large cities will have many small commercial firms dealing with good commercial work, which are not high street firms.

Typically a trainee solicitor in a small firm will have much more client contact from an early stage. You may still be working as part of a team, but normally you will work closely with the supervisor and, upon qualification, you will work autonomously. It is not unusual to have a high degree of responsibility, and even partnership, cast upon you early on.

The financial rewards might not be as high as those in the larger law firms – but smaller law firms tend to offer a different quality of life (i.e. shorter hours) and work that is more related to everyday life. Typical trainee starting salaries are around £18,000 in London and £16,000 outside London. Usually small firms do not offer any support with course fees or maintenance. Once qualified, starting salaries tend to be in the range of £19,000–£27,000 depending on the firm and area of qualification. Smaller firms tend to recruit six to 12 months ahead of when they expect the trainee to commence work with the firm.

Case study

Gavin Henshaw, aged 29, qualified as a solicitor in 2003. He now practises at The Head Partnership just outside Reading and specialises in family law.

'I graduated from Sunderland University with a degree in English studies. Midway through my final year at university I decided I should focus on what I wanted to do in the future and the law appealed.

Immediately thereafter I trained with, and qualified at, a small firm in Chesham. Six months after qualifying I moved to my present firm and, almost four years on, I can say that this was certainly the right decision for me. Whilst I initially thought about working in London, this was never something I seriously wanted. I was more interested in working for a smaller firm where everyone in the office knows everyone else as opposed to merely being a faceless employee. Also, in working for a smaller firm you are actively involved in dealing with cases and clients from a very early stage and, in any event, given the area in which the firm is based, I have found that the standard of the work I deal with is comparable to anything you would encounter in London. For me, my current situation provides me with a great work–life balance and I have no intention of changing this arrangement, as it is far more important to me than any financial advantage that working in London could offer.'

Office-based or in the courtroom?

Traditionally the work of a solicitor has been predominantly office-based, with some undertaking advocacy work in the lower courts (mainly criminal work in the magistrates' court). This is still mainly the case as, in practice, solicitors can earn more money working in the office than they can waiting around at court for cases to be heard. In addition, the typical hourly charge-out rates for solicitors far exceed the average charge-out rates of barristers (for example, it is not uncommon for a junior barrister to earn £150 per day for an appearance, whereas a trainee solicitor may be charged out at over £100 per hour!) – so it is often more economical for the client to instruct a barrister to undertake court work.

Recently solicitors have been able to obtain the same right to be heard in the higher courts as barristers, known as the higher rights of audience. Once a solicitor has obtained experience of advocacy in the lower courts, they can undertake an additional training course and, upon successful completion of it, take up the higher rights of audience. A number of solicitors have taken this path but it is still relatively unusual.

Barristers

One of the complaints about the English legal system is that lawyers are like buses: as soon as one appears, another two or three turn up as well. This impression comes from the fact that solicitors can often employ barristers to give specialist advice or to represent the client in court – so, instead of hiring only one lawyer, the client now has at least two on their hands. This section will outline what barristers do and how their work differs from that of a solicitor.

What's the work like?

Barristers are specialist legal advisors and courtroom advocates: they are lawyers whom other lawyers consult on a specific issue, whether for advice or to make use of their advocacy skills. As suggested in Chapter 1, their work compares to that of consultants or surgeons in the medical profession, whereas the work of a solicitor compares to that of a GP.

Just as the usual route to a consultant is through a referral from a GP, so the usual route to a barrister is through a solicitor (although there are a few exceptions to this – see Chapter 1): the Bar is a referral profession, so members of the public cannot generally directly engage a barrister. Solicitors will have good working relationships with barristers and are likely to know or be able to find out the most suitable barrister to deal with a particular case.

Barristers work as individual practitioners: they cannot form partnerships with other lawyers and are responsible for their own caseload. They do, however, form groups known as chambers or sets in which a number of barristers have their offices in the same building and share the administrative expenses of clerks and facilities – but these are not firms. Every chamber has an experienced barrister at its head; there will be a number of other members of varying seniority – permanent members of a set of chambers are known as tenants and temporary members are known as squatters.

Barristers are independent and objective, and will advise a client on the strengths and weaknesses of the case. Unlike solicitors, they automatically have rights of audience (i.e. the right to appear and present a case) in any court in the land. When a barrister qualifies, it is said that they have been 'called to the Bar', which refers to the bar or rail which used to divide the area of the courtroom used by the judge from the area used by the general public: only barristers were allowed to approach the bar to plead (argue) their clients' cases. The term 'barrister' is derived from this usage of bar.

There are two types of barristers: junior counsel and senior counsel.

Senior counsel are those senior barristers who have been made Queen's Counsel (QC) as a mark of outstanding ability. This is also known as 'taking silk', which refers to the silk gowns they traditionally wear – thus a senior barrister is often referred to as a silk. A QC is therefore a senior barrister who is normally instructed in serious or complex cases and would usually appear only in the higher courts. Most senior judges once practised as QCs.

Junior counsel is the term used to describe all other barristers who have not been made QCs.

Barristers tend to specialise in particular areas of law, for example civil law, family law, criminal law or immigration law. The work of a civil barrister may be divided into two types: contentious and non-contentious. Contentious work involves cases where litigation is contemplated or a real possibility. Non-contentious work involves advising on matters which have arisen not from a dispute between parties but often from a desire to avoid litigation in the future (for example the drafting of a will, the creation of a trust or advising on the terms of a contract).

Why engage a barrister?

A solicitor might want to engage a barrister for two main reasons. First, to gain an opinion on a matter of law from a person who is an expert or specialist in a particular field; second, to represent the client in court where the solicitor is not allowed to or would prefer a specialist advocate to take on the task. A well-argued case will impress a judge; good cross-examination will impress a jury. A barrister's specialist advocacy skills could make a difference to the outcome of a case.

When a solicitor asks for a barrister's view on a legal point it is known as seeking 'counsel's opinion'; where the barrister is asked to undertake litigation work (for example, disputes between individuals) in court it is known as 'instructing or briefing counsel', though the two expressions are often used loosely today. If an opinion is sought the barrister will be sent the relevant paperwork and will research the area of law and consider the issues before expressing a view as to the merits of the case or what steps to take next. In many cases, barristers are able to give advice on a case simply by looking at the papers. In more complex cases, and certainly cases which go to court, it will usually be necessary to have a conference or consultation with the barrister, typically at the barrister's chambers. If counsel is instructed to act then the barrister will begin to prepare his or her arguments that will later be used in court. Thus most of a barrister's work will typically be centred on legal disputes. The barrister acts like the old medieval champion: stepping in to fight in the place of the client.

What makes a good barrister?

'You need to have utter confidence in what you are doing – or at least appear to,' says one newly qualified young barrister. 'You are absolutely vulnerable to the whims of the solicitor. You need to be flexible and robust.' A key skill for a barrister is to persuade, so strong communication skills are high on the list. You also need to be interested in people and business, and to be commercially aware (you will, after all, effectively be running your own small business). Below is a list of skills and qualities you might need:

- commercial awareness
- computer skills
- confidence
- energy and drive
- flexibility and adaptability
- good academic ability
- independence
- interpersonal skills
- meticulousness
- numeracy
- written and verbal communication skills.

Who works where?

There are over 11,500 barristers in self-employed independent practice in England and Wales. Although some do a wide variety of legal work, many focus on particular aspects of litigation and the law, specialising in areas such as construction, property, company law, crime, employment, personal injury, taxation, intellectual property or many other areas.

Barristers also work for the Crown Prosecution Service (CPS), the Government Legal Service and magistrates' courts. Some barristers may hardly ever appear in court but spend their time writing opinions and giving advice on complex and difficult areas of law. Most barristers practise from London but about 5,000 are based in other cities and towns, including Birmingham, Bristol, Cardiff, Leeds, Manchester and Nottingham. All barristers who practise in England and Wales are members of one of the six legal circuits (geographical areas) into which the two countries are divided. The circuits are the areas around which the high court judges travel to hear the most important cases.

Case study

Paul is an experienced barrister who has been working from chambers in London since 1985. Most of his work is with insurers, giving them advice on whether or not they should meet a claim. He deals a lot with recovery work and employers' liability.

'It is very important to build up your reputation. This often starts with your clerk who will recommend you to do a piece of work from solicitors. After that you'll tend to build up your reputation by word of mouth,' says Paul. 'Your task in court is to persuade the tribunal, so good communication skills are vitally important. You also need to communicate effectively with your own clients. A good grasp of the law and the enthusiasm to carry on learning is necessary.'

A lot of stamina is required to be a barrister as the job is very hard work, often requiring you to work more than 10-hour days, sometimes six or seven days a week. 'Working from 6am until midnight is common, especially on a long case which can go on for weeks on end,' says Paul. Because it is a tough profession Paul advises that you should give it serious thought. 'It's a very enjoyable profession. For people who like to be independent and work for themselves it's the ideal profession. But you need to be able to work on your own initiative and find a way of managing your work so that it does not entirely dominate your life'. He says you need a minimum 2:1 degree and advises you to do a mini-pupillage, preferably somewhere you plan to apply for pupillage.

Paralegals and legal secretaries

Working alongside solicitors in firms are various support staff who are not fully qualified lawyers, but depending on the level of qualifications they hold may be able to carry out similar work to solicitors. The terms paralegal, legal secretary and legal assistant are often used to describe such support staff, but there is a difference between a paralegal and a legal secretary.

Paralegals are also known as legal assistants, and will work in law firms carrying out various tasks of a legal nature including advising clients, legal research and drafting documents. Paralegals will often be law graduates who have not moved on to the vocational and professional stages of qualifying as a solicitor or barrister. The paralegal profession is currently unregulated, which means that it is not necessary to have any formal qualifications to become a paralegal, but the Institute of Paralegals is working to develop a nationally recognised paralegal qualifications framework. For more information see www.theiop.org.

Legal secretaries are basically secretaries that work in law firms – i.e. they give administrative support to solicitors. This will include taking telephone calls from clients, typing up letters to clients, invoicing clients, and preparing and filing legal documents. There are no formal qualifications required to become a legal secretary, but good typing, communication and IT skills are the qualities that any firm employing a legal secretary would look for. There are several bodies offering various training courses for legal secretaries, for example the Institute of Legal Secretaries and PAs (www.institutelegalsecretaries.com).

The impact of the recession

The 2008 recession started to hit law firms in the first quarter of 2009, with most large law firms announcing a slowdown in the rate at which trainees were to be taken on. By the third quarter of 2009 most firms had planned a slowdown in recruitment for 12 months.

Firms still place much emphasis on good A level grades in their selection criteria. There is some evidence that employers still look at the 'old' universities or what they perceive to be 'good' universities for their trainees. So in some cases students who had to study at regional universities because of financial constraints may be discriminated against.

More and more students are completing their professional studies part-time, mostly due to the lack of financial support.

In 2009–10 there were 9,000 students on the full-time LPC (Legal Practice Course), an increase of more than 1,800 from the year 2000.

The number of registered two-year training contracts has increased, but due to the 2008 recession the number of new training contracts will be reduced.

For the 2009–10 BPTC (Bar Professional Training Course), about 3,000 applicants applied for 1,600 full-time and 130 part-time places available on the BPTC.

> More paralegals are being recruited to do routine work. This is often seen as a way in for LPC and BPTC students.

The legal profession in Northern Ireland

As in England and Wales, the legal profession in Northern Ireland is divided into the two distinct branches of solicitors and barristers, and these professions have the same roles as in England and Wales. Solicitors in Northern Ireland are regulated by the Law Society of Northern Ireland, and barristers are governed by the General Council of the Bar of Northern Ireland.

> For more information please see: www.barlibrary.com/about-us/the-general-council-of-the-bar-of-northern-ireland or www.lawsoc-ni.org

The legal profession in Scotland

The main difference in the composition of the legal profession in Scotland is that instead of there being the two separate professions of solicitors and barristers, in Scotland there are solicitors and advocates.

Solicitors

As in England and Wales, solicitors in Scotland give advice on a wide variety of areas of law, with individual solicitors specialising in areas that they have been trained in. Solicitors in Scotland can represent clients in the Justice of the Peace and sheriff courts.

Solicitors in Scotland are both represented and regulated by the Law Society of Scotland, which sets standards for the profession, including education and training requirements, and disciplines solicitors where necessary.

Advocates

Advocates (sometimes referred to as 'counsel') are lawyers that are specifically trained in advocacy, so can represent clients in any Scottish court. They are equivalent to barristers in England and Wales, and the relationship between solicitors and advocates works the same as that between solicitors and barristers in England and Wales, in that advocates are usually instructed through a solicitor instead of being instructed directly by individuals.

Advocates are members of the Scottish Bar, and are regulated and represented by the Faculty of Advocates, which carries out similar functions as the Scottish Law Society. The faculty is led by an elected Dean, and the faculty controls its own admissions and discipline. It also trains and prepares candidates for admission to the Bar.

Solicitor advocates

Solicitor advocates are experienced solicitors who have undertaken specialist training in court pleading. Since 1990, they have had rights of audience equal to advocates in the High Court of Justiciary and the Court of Session. They are members of the Law Society of Scotland and are regulated by that body.

Reform of the legal profession in Scotland

The Legal Services (Scotland) Act 2010 makes various changes to the operation of the legal profession in Scotland, although most of the Act is not yet in force and the timetable for implementation is still under discussion.

When it comes into force the Act will reduce the restrictions on solicitors entering into business relationships with non-solicitors, as the Legal Service Act 2007 has allowed solicitors, barristers and non-lawyers to work together in England and Wales.

> For more information on the legal profession in Scotland see www.scotland.gov.uk/Topics/Justice/legal/17822/10190

4| How to qualify as a lawyer

So now we come to the crucial matter: how do you start on the long road to becoming a lawyer? As there are two distinct branches of the legal profession, there are different training routes for each branch. This chapter will start by looking at how to qualify as a solicitor in England and Wales, followed by an overview of how to qualify in Scotland and Northern Ireland, and will then move on to qualifying as a barrister.

Solicitors

It may come as a surprise to learn that there are a number of different routes by which you can qualify as a solicitor. Most of these are set out in the diagram overleaf and then described in more detail in the text that follows.

Before university

A levels

Nearly all A levels provide an acceptable grounding for a law degree. The traditional paper-based subjects such as history and English have an obvious appeal; languages may also prove to be very attractive to employers (particularly if you end up working for a firm with offices overseas) and sciences will develop logical thought and application, which are key skills for any lawyer.

Some top universities have a list of preferred subjects, and, for example, may require applicants to have two of their subjects from this preferred list, but such lists are not generally available to the public. In 2011, for the first time the Russell Group of 20 top UK universities published a document called 'Informed Choices' which provides some guidance on choosing A level subjects. This document is available to download from: www.russellgroup.ac.uk/informed-choices.aspx.

The one A level which does seem to cause some controversy is law. There have been suggestions in the press that A level law is a 'soft' subject, not favoured by universities. However, research published in the *A level Law Review* demonstrates that in reality this is not the case.

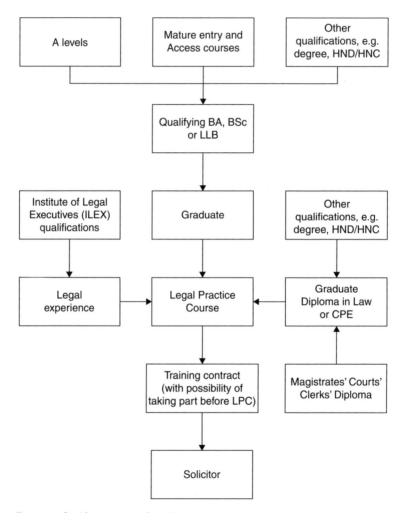

Figure 1: Qualification route for solicitors

The exam board AQA asked universities offering law degrees whether they view A level Law in the same way as other A levels such as English or History, and 81 institutions out of 83 said they did. Institutions responding positively included Cambridge, Oxford, University College London (UCL), King's College London, Edinburgh, Warwick, Birmingham, Nottingham and Durham universities.

The only two institutions that termed A level Law a 'less preferred subject' were the London School of Economics and Political Sciences (LSE) and Manchester University, but both said they would accept A level Law '*so long as it is accompanied by two other subjects that are not on their list of less preferred subjects.*'

A law A level provides a good grounding for a law degree and is a subject that is valued by universities, but if you have concerns then take the following steps.

- If you want to study A level Law and already have a university in mind, check with the admissions department that it would be accepted.
- If you are already studying A level Law but have not yet applied for university then do your research before applying so you know which universities will accept your combination of A level subjects.

Access courses

A number of universities offer Access courses. If you are a mature student who missed out on completing your secondary education, Access courses are designed to help you move into higher education and on to degree-level studies. You may not have the academic qualifications of your fellow students but you will have acquired other skills and qualities in the workplace or at home and these will help you to make the transition to degree studies.

To find out more about Access courses, contact the universities and colleges in your local area to learn what they offer and when their courses run.

The academic stage of training

The law degree

Many universities offer law degrees, and these vary enormously in style and content – for example:

- some are traditional in content
- some enable you to gain real legal clinical experience
- some enable you to obtain a joint degree (e.g. law and languages, law and politics, law and accountancy).

This variety gives you the opportunity to choose the degree which best suits your skills and interests – but if you have any intention of qualifying as a solicitor, you must ensure that your degree is recognised by the Solicitors Regulation Authority (SRA) as a qualifying law degree (QLD) – see Chapter 6 for details. The SRA maintains a list of those institutions whose degrees are recognised as QLDs, so it's easy to check whether your preferred degree is on the list. Having a QLD means that you have studied the subjects which the SRA considers to be the key foundation subjects for any lawyer.

These are:

- contract
- criminal law
- equity and trusts
- European Union law
- land (or property)
- public law (constitutional and administrative)
- tort.

The Law Society stipulates that your study of these subjects must account for about half of your total studies on a three-year law degree and, in total, at least two-thirds of your degree must be spent on law and law-related subjects. Once you begin looking for a training contract (see below), you'll discover that many firms will expect you to have either a First or 2:1 degree. You'll need to work hard right from the outset of your degree to maximise your chances of getting a training contract with the firm of your choice.

The exempting degree

The idea behind the exempting degree is to combine the academic and vocational (see below) stages of training. At the time of going to press, only three exempting law degrees are on offer, at Northumbria University, Huddersfield University and Westminster University: the degrees are four years long and, on completion of your studies, you'll be deemed to have the equivalent of both a QLD (see above) and the Legal Practice Course (see below). The obvious attraction of the exempting degree can be the funding arrangements.

The Graduate Diploma in Law (GDL)

What do you do if your degree is in an area other than law and, on completion of your studies, you decide that your greatest ambition is to qualify as a lawyer? Luckily there is a course which enables you to convert your existing degree to something more relevant. This course is usually known as the Graduate Diploma in Law (GDL) – although you may also hear it referred to as the Common Professional Examination (CPE). It is accepted by both the Bar Council and the SRA, so you can start the GDL without having decided whether you eventually intend to qualify as a solicitor or as a barrister, and then make your decision during the course of your studies.

The GDL is a one-year full-time course offered at around 40 institutions across England and Wales. Many of the same institutions also offer the GDL on a part-time basis over two years and, as with law degrees, the SRA maintains a list of all institutions which offer the GDL and in which modes.

The current cost of a full-time GDL ranges from around £7,000 to £9,000. You should check what the course fee includes – for example, some providers will include the cost of all books and materials within their fees whereas others will expect you to pay for these direct. Remember that you get what you pay for, so do not necessarily opt for the most inexpensive course. Look to see if the course provider has links with the professions.

Application for a full-time GDL course is made via the Central Applications Board (the CAB), which runs a system similar to UCAS. The opening date for applications is usually in November each year and the closing date is the following March; have a look on the CAB website (www.lawcabs.ac.uk) for more information. Application for a part-time GDL course is usually made direct to the institution(s) of your choice.

Case study

Mark was always very clear about his career aspirations but decided that in order to have the option of specialising in intellectual property he needed to complete a science degree as some of the work can involve patents and scientific know-how. He studied chemistry at Imperial College and spent two years in London and two in Paris, where he undertook research and studied some French literature. Having planned with precision, Mark applied to do his CPE at the College of Law in London.

'I wanted to move back to London after Paris and wanted to be at the College, because it has a reputation for quality courses and is well recognised by leading firms. I had already started doing vacation placements at various firms and knew that although I enjoyed the research, long-term I wanted to work in a profession more oriented around people.'

Mark found the CPE very fast-paced and practical, which is excellent for a scientist who has always dealt with the practical applications of his experiments. 'CPE students do miss out a little on discussing the implications of law, but the practical aspects are great and really prepare you for life in a law firm.' Mark had always been part of a debating team, all through school and university, and when he arrived at the College he was keen to help give the debating team a boost. 'Debating introduces you to the skills of presenting your case in a logical way and in public. All solicitors need these skills as they have to talk to clients, think on their feet and justify their actions in an ordered and coherent way.'

The non-graduate route

If you don't possess a degree, there are still a number of options available to you. If you already work in the legal sector, for example as a paralegal or as a legal secretary, you may decide to take the Institute of Legal Executives' examinations. The higher-level examinations are recognised by the SRA as being equivalent to a law degree and will therefore enable you to progress to the next stage of training, the Legal Practice Course (see below).

In exceptional circumstances, the length and quality of your work experience in any field, law or otherwise, may be recognised by the SRA as equivalent to a degree and could therefore permit you to take up a place on a GDL course. For more information on the non-graduate route to qualification contact the SRA, whose staff will be able to give you advice on your circumstances.

The vocational stage of training

The Legal Practice Course (LPC)

Following completion of the academic stage of training, prospective solicitors must complete a Legal Practice Course (LPC) at one of around 35 institutions across England and Wales. The LPC can be completed over one year full time or two years part time (in a variety of formats including evening, weekend or day-release study patterns). The current cost ranges from £9,000 to £13,000 for the full-time course.

The LPC is made up of a combination of compulsory subjects and skills which you must cover regardless of where you do the LPC. You also take three elective subjects which you will be able to choose from the range offered by your chosen institution. The LPC is very different from the academic stage of training: you will spend a lot more time in small groups with other students and the skills content of the course means you will experience more 'learning by doing'.

As for the GDL, application for a full-time LPC course is via the Central Applications Board (www.lawcabs.ac.uk). The opening date for applications is usually in early October and the initial closing date is in early December for courses starting the following September. Applications for part-time courses are made direct to the institution(s) of your choice.

The training contract

The final stage of your route to qualification as a solicitor is the training contract. This is (usually) two years of on-the-job training with a firm or other organisation which has been authorised by the SRA to take trainee solicitors. The SRA will require you to gain experience in at least three distinct areas of law during your training contract and to further develop your legal skills whilst doing so. You will also have to complete the Professional Skills Course (PSC), which includes further training and some assessment in legal skills. Your firm or employer is expected to support you through this process.

Depending on the sort of firm you want to go to for your training contract, you may need to apply up to two years in advance of your possible start date. This is certainly the case with the large City and national corporate and commercial firms, which will be recruiting as you are entering the final year of your law degree studies or starting your GDL. Other firms and organisations will recruit you as you are completing your LPC, with a view to an immediate start, so it is also common for students to start their LPC without knowing if they have a training contract to go to at the end of the course.

You can complete your training contract on a part-time basis and you can also combine your training contract with attendance on a part-time LPC. If you have considerable previous experience in a legal environment, then you may be eligible for a reduction in the length of your training contract, but this will depend on whether your employer supports your request. Any application has to be made to the SRA.

Funding your qualification

Qualifying as a solicitor has become an expensive business and it's not unusual for students to find themselves in around £30,000 of debt at the end of their LPC. So, what are your options?

Sponsorship

Many medium to large firms and other employers will sponsor you through the LPC and possibly the GDL if you have secured your training contract before commencing the course. The sponsorship will cover the cost of the GDL/LPC course fees and often a contribution towards your living expenses. You'll need to check whether the firms and employers that interest you would offer sponsorship of this kind.

The Solicitors Regulation Authority (SRA)

The SRA has a bursary scheme and a Diversity Access Scheme (DAS). The bursary scheme is aimed at students with a place on the GDL or LPC who can demonstrate a clear financial need as well as a commitment to a career as a solicitor. The DAS consists of several elements, one of which is a free places scheme with a number of LPC providers. For more details on both schemes, contact the SRA (www.sra.org.uk).

Access funds

These are available at universities and publicly funded colleges. They are discretionary awards aimed at assisting with your living costs if you are experiencing financial hardship. Details are available direct from your institution of study.

Career development loans

Once you get to the GDL or LPC stage of training, you may be eligible for a career development loan. For more information see www.lifelong-learning.co.uk.

Charities and grant-making trusts

Find out from your local authority whether there are any such bodies in the area where you live and, if there are, check whether you meet their criteria for an award.

When you are looking for sources of funding, remember:

- do your research
- plan ahead
- read the criteria for the grant/award you are applying for and make sure you can demonstrate that you meet them
- don't be put off – you're training to be a solicitor so try to come up with a good case for yourself
- be realistic.

Case study

Karen is a trainee at Lewis Silkin, a medium-sized law firm based in the City of London and renowned for its specialist areas of expertise, in particular employment, advertising and social housing. Karen completed A levels in English Language, Law, Mathematics and General Studies. She obtained three A grades and a B grade. Karen went straight to Bristol University, where she read law. In her first year she studied tort, criminal, public and property law. In her second she chose jurisprudence, contract, property, trusts and European law. In her third she elected to do medicine, law and ethics, intellectual property, revenue law, and gender and the law. She obtained a 2:1.

Karen seemed clear from the start that she wanted to be a solicitor. She comments: 'I wanted to be able to deal with clients from the beginning of a case and because of the possibilities for solicitor advocates nowadays it didn't seem to be closing any doors.

I also dislike the stuffy traditions of the Bar.' Karen obtained a distinction on the LPC.

Karen also made sure that she gained work experience through summer work placements. 'After my second year at university I spent an intensive summer working for White & Case for two weeks, Barlow Lyde & Gilbert for two weeks, Olswang for three weeks and Mirror Group Newspapers (in-house legal department) for one week.' Karen is in her first seat in the employment department at Lewis Silkin. She hopes to proceed to corporate as her next seat. A typical day in the employment department could involve her attending a tribunal, preparing documents for a tribunal hearing, interviewing a witness and drafting the witness statement, attending conference with counsel or assisting in negotiating a settlement or reviewing contractual documents, for example a contract of employment.

There are six trainees per year (that is, 12 at any one time) at Lewis Silkin. The favoured seats for a training contract are corporate, employment, litigation and intellectual property. In addition to the Professional Skills Course (PSC), Lewis Silkin conducts in-house training for its trainees.

There is a good induction programme at Lewis Silkin and a comprehensive system of support, so there is always someone to help you when you need it. However, because of the intense competition for training contracts Karen thinks you really need something to help you stand out. 'Being outgoing, having a sense of humour, and language and computer skills will give you the edge,' she says. 'My legal experience also helped enormously.' She advises, 'You must be very committed before going to law school as costs are great unless you are sponsored. Be focused and persistent.'

Qualifying as a solicitor in Scotland

As outlined in Chapter 2, the legal system in Scotland differs from that of England and Wales and Northern Ireland, and so does the qualification route. It is not possible to go into great detail in this book but below is a summary.

Please note that changes to the system of qualifications for solicitors in Scotland were made from September 2011. The changes are largely to the names of the different stages of qualification, and these have been given in parentheses, but for more information please see www.lawscot. org.uk.

The academic stage

It is possible to study a Bachelor of Law degree (LLB) (Foundation Programme) at the following Scottish universities:

- The University of Aberdeen
- The University of Abertay
- The University of Dundee
- The University of Edinburgh
- The University of Glasgow
- Glasgow Caledonian University
- Napier University
- Robert Gordon University
- The University of Stirling
- The University of Strathclyde.

More detailed information about the content of the LLB degree can be obtained from the law schools at each of the universities by visiting their websites.

The LLB is offered as an Ordinary Degree over three years or an Honours Degree over four years. To obtain a place on an LLB in Scotland you would need in the region of four A grades and one B grade at Higher. Students who already have a degree in another subject can apply for the two-year accelerated degree.

Warning: A law degree from an English university will not be accepted as a qualifying law degree in Scotland, and vice versa. However, if you have qualified in England, Wales, Northern Ireland and other parts of the European Union, there are transfer tests available in order to requalify in Scotland. Information on how to convert qualifications from a different country (e.g. if you qualified in England but want to practise in Scotland) can be found by visiting the websites of the law societies and Bar councils for each country.

The non-graduate route

Alternatively, there is a non-degree route where someone who has been working as a full-time pre-Diploma trainee with a qualified solicitor in Scotland for three years can take the Scottish Law Society's examinations. For more information please see www.lawscot.org.uk/becomingasolicitor/route-to-qualification—requalification/beginning-a-career.

The vocational stage

After completion of the LLB degree all prospective solicitors are required to take the Diploma in Legal Practice (professional education and training stage 1, or PEAT 1), which lasts seven months and can be studied in Aberdeen, Dundee, Edinburgh and Glasgow. This is similar to the Legal Practice Course (LPC) in England and Wales, in that the course has been designed to teach the practical knowledge and skills necessary for the working life of a solicitor. It does, however, slightly differ from the LPC in that most of the teaching of the Diploma is carried out by solicitors and the focus is highly practical and skills-based. To obtain a place on the Diploma course, applicants would need to have passed all of the professional subjects in their LLB (or Law Society examinations).

The post-Diploma training contract

After successful completion of the Degree and Diploma, you need to serve a two-year post-Diploma training contract (professional education and training stage 2, or PEAT 2) with a practising solicitor in Scotland. This can be served with solicitors in private practice, the Crown Office, or local authorities and certain public bodies. The training contract is very similar to that in England and Wales, giving the trainee the chance to put into practice what they learnt at university. At the end of the two years, if the training contract has been successful then the practising solicitor will certify to the Law Society that the trainee is a fit and proper person to become a solicitor, and at that point the trainee can apply for a full practising certificate.

Qualifying as a solicitor in Northern Ireland

The academic stage

Unlike in Scotland, you do not have to have studied your law degree in Northern Ireland, but your law degree must be considered to be a 'recognised law degree'. Details of what constitutes a recognised law degree, and a list of universities whose law degrees count as recognised, can be accessed through www.lawsoc-ni.org/joining-the-legal-profession.

There are also alternative, non-law degree routes available. Please visit the above website for further details.

The vocational stage

The vocational training to become a solicitor in Northern Ireland can be undertaken at either the Institute of Professional Legal Studies, part of Queen's University Belfast, or the Graduate School of Professional Legal Education, part of the University of Ulster. There is a single application procedure for both courses, and all applicants must sit an entrance exam in the December before they wish to commence the course. The main difference from the system in England and Wales, is that applicants must have already found a Master (a solicitor with whom the applicant proposes to serve his/her apprenticeship) by the time they apply for the vocational course.

The apprenticeship

The apprenticeship is similar to a training contract in England and Wales, and will last two years for trainees who completed the traditional qualification route. Each year will be structured as follows.

- September to December: spent in-office.
- January to December: spent at the Institute of Professional Legal Studies or the Graduate School of Professional Legal Education.
- January to August: spent in-office.

Once a trainee has passed all the relevant examinations and completed their apprenticeship, they can apply to be enrolled as a solicitor of the Court of Judicature in Northern Ireland and apply for a Practising Certificate.

For more information on qualifying as a solicitor in Northern Ireland, please see www.lawsoc-ni.org/joining-the-legal-profession.

Barristers

The academic stage required to become a barrister is the same as that required to become a solicitor. It is only once a student reaches the vocational stage of training that the qualification routes vary for solicitors and barristers. Please see the notes above in the qualifying as a solicitor section for details on A levels, law degrees, and the Graduate Diploma in Law. The only point to bear in mind for students wishing to become barristers as opposed to solicitors, is that it is going to be very difficult to obtain a pupillage (see below) unless you achieve at least a 2:1 at degree level.

The vocational stage

To become a barrister entitled to practise, the Bar Council requires you to take the one-year (full-time) or two-year (part-time) Bar Professional Training Course (BPTC), previously known as the Bar Vocational Course (BVC). Before you start the BPTC you will need to join one of the four Inns of Court: Lincoln's Inn, Inner Temple, Middle Temple or Gray's Inn (all based in central London). These provide collegiate activities, support for barristers and student members, advocacy training and other continuing professional development opportunities. The Inns also provide the mechanism by which students become barristers, known as 'call to the Bar', once they have completed the BPTC and pupillage. The BPTC aims to help you gain the skills of advocacy, conference skills, drafting, legal research, negotiation and opinion writing to prepare you for the practical stage of training on the job, the one year of pupillage. It is available at 11 different teaching institutions throughout the country:

1. Nottingham Law School
2. The College of Law, London
3. The College of Law, Birmingham
4. BPP Law School, London
5. BPP Law School, Leeds
6. Kaplan Law School
7. The University of West England, Bristol
8. Cardiff Law School
9. Manchester Metropolitan University
10. Northumbria University
11. City Law School.

Pupillage

Pupillage is the final stage to qualifying as a barrister and is hard work. The first six months of pupillage are non-practising and involve training with a senior barrister (your 'pupil master') at work for six months (unpaid). During the first six months you will be expected to undertake legal research, draft opinions, and read your pupil master's paperwork.

Once you have completed the first six months, you will spend the second six months practising and be able to appear in court as an advocate. This is when you start to build your own reputation and have your own cases.

Those of you eager to become a barrister are in for a tough time. Competition for places is keen. In the 2009–10 academic year there were only 460 pupillages available. On completion of the BPTC, a high proportion of people will be unable to get pupillage but may be able to work for a legal department in a major company.

In 2001, the Bar Council introduced a new pupillage application system. All pupillage vacancies are now advertised on the OLPAS (Online Pupillage Application System) website accessed through the Pupillage Portal (www.pupillages.com). Before applying find out as much as possible about your preferred set of chambers. You can access the chamber's website or online Bar Directory, or attend a pupillage fair.

Case study

Kim ran her own prosperous car spraying business for five years before deciding to embark on the long and uncertain route to the Bar. She successfully completed the BVC at the College of Law and is now on her first six-month pupillage. Why was Kim so determined to become a barrister? 'One of the options in my Institute of the Motor Industry exams focused on law and I've been fascinated by it ever since. The experiences of a friend who is a barrister also inspired me – what also appealed was the variety of work you deal with, being self-employed and the challenges that the Bar presents.' Kim gave up her business to undertake a law degree at Middlesex University as a mature student. She was keen to gain experience from different sets of chambers.

'I prepared early and spent a lot of time during the third year of university applying for mini-pupillages – I did 14 before starting at the College of Law. It gave me the ideal opportunity to learn about different chambers, what kind of work they do and how they function.' Kim chose to study the BVC at the College the first year the course was offered. 'The course was opening up to new providers and I wanted to be part of the innovative teaching methods that were being offered by the College. I also chose the College of Law because of its reputation in the legal community.'

The BVC was a challenge. The sheer volume of work and the fact that she was constantly learning new skills made it hard, but also rewarding. 'Overall I really enjoyed the course. It was hard work, especially learning new skills such as drafting and opinion writing. Everything had a practical approach, which is different from most academic study. We also worked in small groups, which was an excellent way to practise these new skills.'

Funding your qualification

Money is an extra hurdle. You'll need a fair amount of it to see you through since the fees alone for the BPTC are in the region of £10,000–£16,000. Those without a qualifying law degree will have an extra year's training to pay for when studying for the Graduate Diploma in Law, and the changes to the fees and funding system for universities from 2012 are going to significantly increase the cost of qualifying (see Chapter 11).

The average cost of completing the vocational stage of training is estimated at over £20,000 if living expenses are taken into account. Only a limited number of awards, grants and scholarships are available for the vocational stage of Bar training. Please refer to the chambers, pupillage and awards handbooks and to the Bar Council Scholarship Trust – further details can be obtained from the Bar Council.

Case study

Claire is a barrister at Blackstone Chambers specialising in employment law. She was called to the Bar in 1998 and secured a tenancy with Blackstone that same year. She studied for A levels in French, Russian and Latin and obtained three A grades. Claire read for a BA in Law (European Option) at Queen's College, Cambridge, spending her third year at the University of Poitiers, France. She got a 2:1 in her first year and a First in her final year. She later completed a master's in Law at Harvard, doing a mixture of antitrust and constitutional law/civil liberties.

Before going to Harvard Claire took a year off. 'After I left college I wasn't sure I wanted to practise law, so I spent a year working for Lord Lester of Herne Hill QC, doing political research and writing speeches on various topics such as human rights and discrimination. I then decided that the Bar probably was for me, so I went to Bar School.

'In the summers after my second and third years at college I spent time at Simmons & Simmons in Paris, Baker & McKenzie in London, Freshfields in London, and Coudert Brothers in London, because at that stage I thought I wanted to use my languages and possibly work in an overseas office. I then decided to go to the Bar instead, and spent time before my fourth year at Monckton Chambers and Brick Court Chambers. During Bar School I did mini-pupillages at 2 Temple Gardens, Monckton Chambers, Brick Court Chambers, Essex Court Chambers and Blackstone Chambers.'

Claire found her summer experience to be invaluable not only in giving her CV further credibility but also in helping her decide whether to be a solicitor or a barrister. 'I initially thought I wanted to use my languages, and being a solicitor was the only realistic option if I wanted to live abroad and still practise law. Having done a number of summer placements, however, I realised that I was perhaps not ideally suited to working in a corporate environment. I also wanted the chance, having formulated the arguments in a case, to be able to put them to a judge, and was concerned that if I did not at least try to become a barrister I might always have wondered what it would have been like. Finally, having decided, more or less on the eve of having to fill in the application forms for solicitors' firms, that I wanted to try the Bar instead, I spoke to my Dad who suggested that the Bar was too uncertain and a bad career for a woman. There was no better way of ensuring that his extremely stubborn daughter would choose the Bar.

'When I was at Bar School there was only one option, namely the ICSL (Inns of Court School of Law). I spent a lot of my time that year doing part-time research jobs to cover the cost of the year over and above the scholarship which my Inn had generously given me, so I probably didn't give the ICSL a fair chance. In general, however, it was not a particularly interesting year.'

Claire's interest in human rights began at college, and her work experience with Lord Lester dealing with public law assisted her decision to focus on public law and employment law. 'I knew a little bit about Blackstone Chambers from my work with Lord Lester, and at the time I was applying for pupillage there were few chambers which were as good as Blackstone concentrating on commercial, employment and public law. Finally, when I came for a mini-pupillage I liked the atmosphere, particularly amongst the junior tenants. You need to enjoy spending time with your colleagues in every profession, but in view of the size of most chambers, and the slow rate of turnover, you have to be really sure that these are people you would enjoy going for a drink with.'

A typical day or week for Claire varies greatly depending on whether she is in court or in a tribunal – last week involved a conference with a QC about disclosure of the electoral roll and the ECHR; drafting an originating application to an employment tribunal in an unfair dismissal case; drafting grounds of resistance for a company on the other side of a similar case; settling a long-standing disability discrimination case for an applicant shortly before the hearing; preparing a judicial review for the Legal Services Commission; and preparing a possible injunction with a QC to enforce restrictive covenants against an ex-employee. It also involved various bits and pieces of advisory work, including advising on witness statements for a forthcoming seven-day disability discrimination hearing. Her hours are irregular and she frequently works in the evenings and at the weekend.

Qualifying as an advocate in Scotland

The academic and vocational stages are the same as qualifying as a solicitor in Scotland (see the section on 'Qualifying as a solicitor in Scotland' on page 37). The intending advocate in Scotland needs to take an LLB degree followed by the postgraduate Diploma in Legal Practice plus one or two years' training in Scotland in a solicitor's office. It is advised that prospective advocates practise as solicitors for a period before going to the Bar.

This is followed by further unpaid practical training called 'devilling' (work-shadowing) to an experienced advocate, in combination with sitting the Faculty of Advocates' written examinations. Please visit the Faculty of Advocates website for more information: www.advocates. org.uk/training/index.html.

Qualifying as a barrister in Northern Ireland

The academic stage is the same as for qualifying as a solicitor; students must have completed a qualifying law degree (see the section on 'Qualifying as a solicitor in Northern Ireland' on page 39).

The vocational stage

Students must undertake the one year full-time Degree of Barrister-at-Law at the Institute of Professional Legal Studies at Queen's University Belfast.

Pupillage

Students are called to the Bar of Northern Ireland after they have passed the Degree of Barrister-at-Law. A person intending to practise at the Bar of Northern Ireland must then enter into pupillage with a barrister for a period of 12 months.

Please visit the following website for more information: www.barlibrary. com/about-barristers/barristers-profession/become-a-barrister.

5 | Getting work experience

Getting work experience is crucial in terms of helping you secure a training contract or pupillage in today's extremely competitive climate. It is not enough to be purely a brilliant academic. The more relevant experience you have, the better the chance of succeeding. You can apply for work experience at any stage in the qualification process, whether it be during A levels, during a law (or other) degree, or even at a later stage if you are having trouble obtaining a training contract or pupillage.

What have you got to gain from work experience?

- It will give you a real insight into the profession and whether or not that is what you want to do. Some real experience will be particularly useful if you are trying to weigh up the pros and cons of qualifying as a barrister or solicitor.
- It helps you to make a better transition into your eventual move into the world of full-time work.
- It gives you the opportunity to build up those all-important contacts.
- It will help you to gain excellent references (hopefully!).

However, it is not that easy getting legal work experience, and can in itself be a competitive process. Most universities and employers recognise this and do not stipulate that work experience is essential, although it is preferred. If you can't get experience in a firm of solicitors or chambers, any work experience that demonstrates use of the skills they are interested in will be valuable. Skills such as communication, determination, business awareness and IT can all be developed in many other sectors of business and commerce. You can also gain relevant experience and knowledge at university and/or BPTC by participating in debating, mooting, Inn advocacy weekends, mock trials and reading the legal pages in newspapers regularly.

Where to apply for work experience

- Placement in a firm of solicitors
- Mini-pupillage in chambers
- Paralegals and outdoor clerks
- Barrister's clerk
- The Law Commission
- Law centres
- Citizens Advice Bureaux
- Voluntary work in charitable organisations.

Marketing yourself

There is no one guaranteed way of succeeding in getting work experience, so try as many as you can think of and be creative in the process. Here are a few suggestions.

- Ask your teachers at school/college if they have any contacts in the legal profession.
- Use your careers service and speak to your careers officer.
- Talk to your family and friends and ask them if they can suggest anyone to contact.
- Make sure everyone you know is aware you are looking for work experience.
- Send your CV to firms of solicitors. The Chambers and Partners directory will give you names and addresses of solicitors' firms.
- Send your CV to chambers. The Chambers and Partners directory will give you names and addresses of chambers.
- Keep up to date with the profession by reading the 'quality press' on their relevant legal days and look at specialist journals such as *The Law Society Gazette* and *The Lawyer*, which should both be available from large public libraries.

Perhaps you could ask to go in for one or two weeks' work experience during the holidays or even ask for one day's work-shadowing to get an insight into what the working environment is like. Whichever route you take will almost certainly be on a voluntary basis (i.e. unpaid) unless you have specific skills to offer, such as good office and keyboard skills, in which case you could try to get some paid work with a firm of solicitors during the summer or register with an employment agency.

How to apply

It's never too early to start to put together a CV. This is a summary of what you have done in your life to date, so if you have hardly any work experience then one page on good quality A4 paper will be sufficient. If you are a mature student with a lot of jobs behind you there is sometimes a case for going onto a second page. So what should go into your CV? Here are the main headings:

- name
- address and telephone number
- date of birth
- nationality
- education and qualifications.

Make sure to include the following points.

Education

Start with your present course of study and work back to the beginning of secondary school. No primary schools please! List the qualifications with grades you already have and the ones you intend to sit.

Work experience

Start with the most recent. Don't worry if you've only had a Saturday job at the local shop or a paper round. Put it all down and try to draw out any relevant skills you have gained from it. Employers would rather see that you've done something.

Skills

List those such as computer skills, software packages used, languages, driving licence.

Interests and positions of responsibility

What do you like to do in your spare time? If you are or have been captain of a sports team, been a committee member or even head boy or head girl at school, put it all down.

Referees

Usually two: an academic referee such as a teacher or head of your school plus someone who knows you well personally, who is not a relative, such as someone you have worked for.

Tips for your CV

There is no standard CV but there is a sample overleaf.

A sample CV

PERSONAL DETAILS

Name	Simon Anthony Tate
Address	134 Hillhouse Avenue
	Portsmouth PO1 2TQ
Telephone No	01234 567890
Date of Birth	10 June 1991
Nationality	British

EDUCATION & QUALIFICATIONS

2003–present   Linfield High School, Portsmouth
A levels English, History, French
GCSEs English (A), Mathematics (B),
History (A), Geography (C),
Chemistry (B), Biology (B),
French (A), Latin (A)

WORK EXPERIENCE

2004 & 2005 Delivering newspapers and magazines throughout my local area

2006 & 2007 (Saturdays) Sales assistant in busy dry cleaners in centre of Portsmouth

August 2007 Two weeks as a temporary receptionist in a small firm of accountants, responsible for answering telephone and general clerical work

SKILLS

Languages – good written and spoken French
Computing – competent in MS Word and Excel

POSITIONS OF RESPONSIBILITY

Captain of football team at school

INTERESTS

Football, swimming, reading (particularly Jane Austen), and travelling to other countries such as America and France

REFERENCES

Available on request

You should also ensure that you do the following.

- Always highlight your good points on a CV and don't leave gaps.
- Always account for your time. If something such as illness prevented you from reaching your potential in your exams, point this out in the covering letter (see below). Lawyers have excellent attention to detail so make sure your spelling and grammar are perfect!

The covering letter

Every CV or application form should always be accompanied by a covering letter. The letter is important because it is usually the first thing a potential employer reads.

Here are some tips.

- The letter should be on the same A4 plain paper as your CV and should look like a professional document. No lined paper please! One side of A4 only.
- Try to find out the name of the person to whom you should send your letter and CV. It makes a great difference to the reader if you can personalise your application. If you start the letter 'Dear Mr Brown', remember you should finish it 'Yours sincerely'.
- The first paragraph should tell the reader why you are contacting them.
- The second paragraph should give them some information to make them interested in you, e.g. highlighting your interest in law along with some specific IT skills.
- Say in the letter if you already know anything about the firm or have read anything in the press recently that was relevant.
- Employers accept typed letters, unless they specifically request one to be handwritten.

A sample covering letter is shown below.

Dear Mr Smith,

I would be very interested in applying for some work experience at Herbert Smith LLP, and wondered whether you would have any such opportunity available. I am currently in the second year of my LLB at Sussex University, and would relish the chance to gain some practical experience during the forthcoming summer break.

From looking at your website I can see that Herbert Smith has an outstanding reputation for dealing with high-value commercial transactions, and this is an area of law that I am particularly interested in, having chosen to study commercial law as an option in my third year. As part of my degree, I have become proficient at conducting legal research, including using databases such as Lexis. I also have strong IT and typing skills, as well as good communication skills that I have built upon by taking part in debates at university.

Please do not hesitate to contact me if you require any further information or would like details of a referee.

Yours sincerely,

Simon Tate

Case study

Laura studied law and criminology at The University of Kent, Canterbury, graduating with a 2:1 in 2008.

'During my time at university I took part in several activities that I thought interviewers would focus on when I began looking for work after Law School. I worked part time at the university Law Clinic. This only took up a few hours every fortnight but allowed me to gain practical experience of working within a functioning law firm as well as developing my ability to work alongside profession-als and interacting with clients. I undertook several other periods of work experience, including a mini-pupillage. Each period of work experience helped me to decide on which area of law I would eventually like to work within as well as allowing me to make important contacts within the profession. Along with my house-mates I also started a social society that raised lots of money for charities, and during training contract interviews this was always commented on.

I then completed the Legal Practice Course at the Guildford Col-lege of Law in 2009. During this year I completed a voluntary course on Legal Aid, as having decided that I would like to practise either family or criminal law, I knew that the majority of my clients would be publicly funded. I also volunteered at the local domestic violence centre as a McKenzie Friend which developed my ability to deal sensitively with clients.

During my time at The College of Law I utilised their careers ser-vice. They helped me to prepare my CV and to practise my inter-view techniques. I also applied for several jobs advertised on their website. I was then offered a training contract with one of these firms. I started my training contract in 2009 and completed seats in their criminal, private client and family departments. I have recently qualified and have been offered a full-time position in their criminal department.

Although good academic results are obviously important I cannot stress how important it is to show a keen interest in the area you wish to work in, show willingness to invest your time and treat every period of work experience or voluntary work as an inter-view.'

6 | Choosing your university law course

In the late 1980s, demand for trainee solicitors briefly exceeded supply. Virtually anyone could pick up a training contract (then called 'articles') if they had the necessary qualifications. These days, however, competition is tough, and you'll need to show lots of ability and drive to impress your potential employers. The situation for budding barristers is even more competitive.

But there is a positive side.

Employers are generally impressed by a good calibre law graduate since law is known to be a challenging discipline requiring skills such as research, analysis, application, clarity, advocacy and effective written communication. These are very relevant in other jobs, so on the one hand you don't need a law degree to enter the profession, but on the other, law can be your springboard into a wide range of career possibilities.

Some parts of the legal profession are growing, with law firms becoming more international and opening offices overseas (particularly in Eastern Europe) and expanding in areas such as environmental law and intellectual property law. The road to qualifying as a barrister or solicitor may not be easy, but the professional rewards can be great. If you are undeterred and still have your heart set on a law degree in some shape or form, then it's time to start thinking about your next steps. Please note that this chapter only offers advice on choosing a law degree. For more general advice on choosing degree courses, please refer to some of the guides mentioned in Chapter 12.

What to consider

The basic criteria for choosing your degree course are:

- the kind of law course you are after
- where you want to study
- your academic ability.

Going to university is an investment, so it is worth giving these points some careful thought. From the growing number of institutions offering law courses you will need to look at ways of narrowing down your options. Once you have eliminated the bulk of the institutions and courses on offer, start to carry out your own research.

Online

Most of the information you would need to know about universities you are interested in applying to is now available online either through UCAS (www.ucas.com) or on the websites of individual universities. Most universities have their prospectuses online or available to download, and there should also be information on who to contact if you have a specific question.

Open days

Attend university open days if you can, and talk to former or current students. Try to imagine whether you would be happy living for three years in that environment and address issues such as: Is it a campus or in a city? Will it allow you to pursue your interests?

Take soundings

Talk to any legal practitioners you know and ask for their views on the reputations of different universities and courses.

Academic achievement

Find out what academic criteria they are looking for and be realistic about the grades you are expecting. Your teachers at school or college will be able to advise you on this. Once you have done this you should be able to produce a shortlist of universities and from that you can choose the top five places to put down in your UCAS application.

Different kinds of law courses available

Qualifying law degrees are recognised by the Law Society and the Bar Council, and only qualifying law degrees allow students to progress to the vocational stage of training. A list of the institutions that offer qualifying law degrees can be found at www.sra.org.uk/students.

This means that you can select the required courses that will exempt you from taking the Graduate Diploma in Law (GDL) after you graduate. The UCAS course code for this type of course is usually M100. The seven foundations of legal knowledge are:

1   contract
2   tort (often both are referred to as obligations)
3   criminal law
4   constitutional and administrative law (or public law)
5   property law (or land law)
6   equity and trusts
7   law of the European Union.

See the glossary for an explanation of these terms.

Single or Joint Honours?

Law can be taken on its own or mixed with a number of other subjects. It can be difficult to decide whether to study law by itself (a Single Honours degree), with another subject (Joint or Combined degree) or as part of a modular programme, alongside a multitude of topics.

If you are considering a Single Honours course, a good range of optional subjects might make it even more inviting. You don't want to be stuck with just a handful of choices from which to fill in your timetable after you've put down the core courses. Options may be law-related or from a completely different discipline. Some institutions can only offer a limited selection, while others provide a variety of law courses as well as the opportunities to take non-law courses. If there is a particular area of law you are interested in, for example human rights law, then you may want to apply to a university that offers this as an option.

Alternatively, if you want to specialise in one other area, then a Joint degree might be more appealing. Some Joint degrees do not require previous knowledge of the second subject. Others, especially those with a European language, often specify that candidates must have an A level or GCSE for background knowledge.

With Joint degrees, be wary of courses that have seemingly identical titles, for example, law with German, law and German, and law and German law. In the first one, law is the major subject; in the second, you'll probably spend equal time on each and in the third the emphasis is on law rather than German language. Any of them may involve some time abroad. It is important to check that any Joint degree counts as a qualifying law degree (see above) if you want to go on to be a solicitor or barrister.

Black Letter, contextual and vocational approaches

It is worth knowing that there are broadly three different approaches to teaching law – but you cannot base your selection on this criterion since few institutions adhere to one kind. Most places are likely to opt for a mixture (sometimes even within an individual unit, especially if it is taught by several different tutors). It can be useful, though, to find out (perhaps during an open day) which attitude is prevalent. The categories are detailed below.

Black Letter law

This focuses on the core subjects and doesn't look much beyond statutes and legal reports for its sources of law. It may sound dry, but it should provide a thorough grounding in the English legal system.

Contextual approach

Some courses examine law in context; that is to say, law, its role and its effectiveness are looked at in relation to society (past and present), politics and the economy. Such courses may include elements of critical legal theory. Students are expected to analyse the problems (for example, loopholes, contradictions, injustices and so on) within the law. This can make for some heated and controversial seminars.

Vocational approach

This stresses professional training and skills. It includes sandwich degrees with work placements, and other degrees with units dedicated to lawyers' skills such as negotiating, interviewing, counselling, drafting, research, analysis, clear expression and the ability to read through vast amounts of material, sift out the legally relevant points and present a logical argument. Ironically, you will be able to pick up most of these skills through other standard law units and extra-curricular activities such as mooting (a mock courtroom trial), debating and law clinics, in which students get the opportunity to help out with a real-life case from start to finish.

Studying overseas and work placements

Studying overseas and/or completing a work placement could also be factors affecting your degree selection. Not all of these courses will send you off for a full year, though. Neither must you be a linguist, since you can study or work overseas in English in, for example, North America, the Netherlands or Malaysia. The availability of student exchanges has increased through programmes such as Erasmus, which encourage universities to provide international opportunities where practicable.

There are relatively few law degree courses which insist on work placements; however, some hands-on experience during holidays will prove invaluable and you should try to organise this yourself even if it is not a requirement of the course you choose (see the previous chapter).

Where you want to study

Which country and legal system?

If you're hoping to practise law, then ask yourself where you intend to work – England or Wales? Northern Ireland? Scotland? Since the legal systems differ throughout the UK, it seems pointless to study in Aberdeen if you want to practise in Aberystwyth (although, if you do need to move, then it is usually possible to transfer the legal skills and knowledge you already have and adapt them to the new location). Information on how to convert qualifications from a different country (e.g. if you qualified in England but want to practise in Scotland) can be found by visiting the websites of the Law Societies and Bar Councils for each country mentioned in Chapter 3. More detail on the differences between the professions in each of the UK countries can be found in Chapters 2 and 3.

Various influencing factors

Once you've decided which country you'll be in, you can think about choosing specific institutions. Remember, university life isn't going to be solely about academic study. It is truly a growing experience – educationally, socially, culturally – and besides, three or four years can really drag if you're not happy outside the lecture theatre. Below is an assortment of factors which might have some bearing on where you'd like to study. See which ones you think are relevant to you and try to put them in order of importance.

Educational facilities

Is there a well-stocked and up-to-date law library nearby or will you have to fight other law students for the materials? Check for computer resources and internet connections, and availability of legal databases (such as Justis and Lexis). More vocational courses might also use mock courtrooms with video and audio equipment. The facilities available will depend on the budget of an institution, and plentiful resources tend to attract better tutors.

Quality of teaching

This is difficult to establish without the benefit of an open day but the Higher Education Funding Council, an independent body set up by the government, has done the groundwork for you and assessed the level of teaching across the UK already. Their findings are publicly available from www.hefce.ac.uk.

League tables of universities for each subject are also published by several organisations, the *Guardian* being one of them. The *Guardian*

University Guide 2012 for law is available at www.guardian.co.uk/education/table/2011/may/17/university-guide-law.

The National Student Survey is also conducted each year to get feedback from students who have studied at university, and is more focused on overall student satisfaction. The results of the survey are published on the following website: http://unistats.direct.gov.uk.

Teaching quality may suffer if seminar or tutorial groups are too large, so try to compare group sizes for the same courses at different institutions.

Type of institution

There are basically three types.

1. **'Old' universities.** Traditionally the more academic universities with higher admission requirements, the old universities are well established with good libraries and research facilities. They have a reputation for being resistant to change, but most are introducing modern elements into their degrees such as modular courses, an academic year split into two semesters, and programmes such as Erasmus.
2. **'New' universities.** Pre-1992 these were polytechnics or institutes. They form a separate group because they still hold true to the original polytechnic doctrine of vocational courses and strong ties with industry, typically through placements and work experience. They are still looked down upon by some employers because of their generally lower academic entry requirements, but the new universities have a good name for flexible admissions and learning, modern approaches to their degrees and good pastoral care. Some law courses at these 'new' universities have been categorised as 'excellent' by the Higher Education Funding Council.
3. **Colleges of higher education.** Usually these are specialist institutions and therefore provide excellent facilities in their chosen fields despite their size. They are sometimes affiliated to universities (such as Holborn College). This form of franchising means the college buys the right to teach the degree, which the university will award, provided that the course meets the standards set by the university.

Attractiveness to employers

Few employers will openly admit to giving preference to graduates from particular universities. Most are looking for high-quality degrees as an indication of strong academic ability. But since students with higher A level grades have tended to go to the old universities, it is unsurprising that a large proportion of successful lawyers come from traditional university backgrounds.

Full time versus part time and distance learning

Although most students prefer to study full time and finish their degrees in the shortest time possible, some people, for a variety of reasons, find it more convenient to study part time or from home or via the internet. Only a limited number of institutions offer these options and they are listed in the guide in Chapter 3.

Guaranteed place on LPC

Many universities have an arrangement with the College of Law which assures a place on an LPC to every student with a 2:2 degree or better. This is a good safety net to have if you fail to get a 2:1, but if you think you will have a problem getting a good law degree before you even start, then ask yourself if you wouldn't be happier and more successful studying another subject.

Non-academic considerations

- **Finances.** The cost of living isn't the same throughout the UK, so will you be able to reach deeper into your pockets for rent or other fundamentals and entertainment if you are living in a major city or in the south?
- **Friends and family.** Do you want to get away from them or stay as close as possible? While there can be advantages, financial at least, to living at home, you may prefer the challenge of looking after yourself and the opportunity to be completely independent.
- **Accommodation.** Do you want to live on campus or in halls of residence with other students, or in private housing that you may need to organise yourself and that could be a considerable distance from college? If your university is nearby, is there any point in moving away from home?
- **Entertainment.** Are you going to be spending much time in, for example, the sports centre, the theatre or student bars? How about university societies: is there one that allows you to indulge your existing hobbies or the ones you've always dreamt of trying?
- **Site and size.** This is not usually a problem since many universities overcome the issue of urban versus rural and small versus large by locating their campus on the edge of a major town (for example the University of Nottingham and the University of Kent), and centralising certain facilities and services to ensure safety, convenience and some sense of community even on the largest and most widespread campus.

Academic ability

For the majority of students, their A level scores will be the deciding criteria for selection. It's important to be realistic about the grades you're heading for: don't be too pessimistic, but don't kid yourself about your 'as yet undiscovered' genius. Talk to your teachers for an accurate picture of your predicted results.

The vast majority of universities offering qualifying law degrees are requiring applicants to have at least three A levels (some even requiring a fourth AS level) and the grade requirements have become even more challenging since the introduction of the A* grade. For example, Cambridge offers are in the region of A*AA (although they may vary) and the University of Sussex usually requires AAB. Information on the entry requirements for law degrees at different universities is available through UCAS or the websites of individual universities.

No institutions require A level Law from potential students, although students who have studied A level Law will obviously find the knowledge they gained at A level to be a useful foundation. Few courses specify subjects they want you to have studied (with the exception of most language Joint degrees), although traditional qualifications are welcomed everywhere. Conversely, some universities won't accept A levels such as General Studies, or the less academic ones such as Art. See Chapter 3 for more information on A level subject choices.

If your A level results effectively prevent you from taking a law degree, then it's time for a rethink. If you wanted to take a law degree with a view to entering the profession, then you could opt for the entry route with a non-law degree instead. Most employers stress that a large number of trainee solicitors and pupil barristers have a non-law degree.

Even though the route might be longer and therefore more expensive (if sponsorship cannot be found), a graduate with, say, a 2:1 Honours degree in philosophy is infinitely more likely to make a successful lawyer than someone who scraped a pass in their LLB. It is important to remember that since degree courses can change format frequently, you must check with universities directly to confirm their specific requirements.

Remember that if you intend to read a subject other than law, you will have to complete the Graduate Diploma in Law before going on to the Legal Practice Course or Bar Professional Training Course.

7 | The UCAS application and the LNAT

So you have chosen a few universities that you would like to apply to study a law degree at; now what? This chapter will guide you through the UCAS application process, and then give you some hints and tips if you are applying to any universities that require the LNAT entrance exam.

Suggested application timescale

Year 12

May/June. Do some serious thinking. Get ideas from friends, relatives, teachers, books, etc. If possible visit some campuses.

June/July. Make a shortlist of your courses.

August. Look at university department websites, download prospectuses and department brochures, find out when open days are being held and try to attend several over the next few months.

Year 13

September. Complete your application and send it off to UCAS – it will be accepted from 1 September onwards.

15 October. Deadline for applying for places at Oxford or Cambridge.

15 January. Deadline for submitting your applications to UCAS. They will consider late applications, but your chances are limited since some of the places will have gone already.

February–April. Interviews may be held.

March. If you have been rejected by all of your choices, you can enter UCAS Extra, a scheme that allows you to apply to other universities. Contact UCAS (www.ucas.com) for details.

April. Decisions will begin to go directly to the candidates.

May. By 15 May, or within two weeks of the final decision you receive, you must tell UCAS (assuming you've had some offers) which offer you have accepted firmly and which one is your back-up.

Spring. Fill in yet more forms – this time the grant forms which you can get from your school, college or local authority.

Summer. Sit your exams and wait for the results.

Results day. If you got the grades, well done! UCAS will send you confirmation (in August) of your place in September. If you missed your grades, don't be too disappointed. Clearing starts straight away so don't waste any time – get hold of a list of unfilled places and contact the universities direct. You will be sent instructions on Clearing automatically. UCAS has now introduced a new scheme called Adjustment which allows students who have performed significantly better than they had expected a short period to approach universities that require higher grades than the offer they were holding. See Chapter 10 for more information on your options.

The UCAS form

The online UCAS form is accessed through the UCAS website (www.ucas.com). You can either register through your school or college, or as a private individual. The UCAS form has six sections that you need to fill out.

1. Personal details: name, address, nationality, etc.
2. Choices: universities and courses you wish to apply for.
3. Education: including exam results and exams to be taken.
4. Employment: including part-time work.
5. Personal statement: see below.
6. Reference: this is usually written by your school or college, but private candidates can get employers or other contacts to write this.

> General advice on filling in your UCAS application is given in another guide in this series, *How to Complete Your UCAS Application* (Trotman, 2012).

Your personal statement

The personal statement section of the UCAS application is the only chance you get to recommend yourself as a serious candidate worthy of a place, or at least worthy of an interview. It is therefore vital that you think very carefully indeed about how to complete it so that it shows you in the best possible light. You must sell yourself to the department of law and make it hard for them not to take you.

There can often be in excess of 20 applicants per place at some universities offering law degrees, so you can understand how competitive applying for law is. Some applicants are able to gain places through Clearing, and a high proportion of applicants do not get places at their first choice universities. However, a good personal statement can help persuade a university to accept you even if you miss the grades required.

Obviously, there are as many ways of writing a personal statement as there are candidates. There are no rules as such, but there are recommendations that can be made. Universities are academic institutions and thus you must present yourself as a strong academic bet. The admissions tutor reading your form will want to know all the relevant information about you and will want some answers to the following questions.

- What is the strength of your commitment to academic study?
- Why do you wish to study law? Money, status, family traditions, the sound of your own voice and legal paraphernalia are not good reasons.
- What precisely is it about the law that interests you? Give details and examples, referring to recent cases, controversies and debates.
- What do you hope to get out of three years of legal academic study?
- What legal cases have you followed in detail?
- What related material have you recently read and why did you appreciate it?
- What recent judgements have you admired and why?
- What legal controversies have excited you?
- Which particular branch of the law interests you most and, again, why?
- Which lawyers, either living or dead, have inspired you and for what reason?

Work experience is very useful as it demonstrates a commitment to the subject outside the classroom, so remember to mention any experience, paid or voluntary. Explain concisely what your job entailed and what you got out of the whole experience. Even if you haven't been able to get work experience, if you have spoken to anyone in the legal profession about their job, then it is worth mentioning as it all builds up a picture of someone who is keen and has done some research. Wanting to be like the characters in legal dramas is not a good enough reason to convince a hardened admissions tutor of your commitment to a law degree!

Future plans, if any, should also be included on your form. Be precise. Again this will demonstrate a breadth of interest in the subject. For example: 'I am particularly interested in pursuing a career at the Bar. My enthusiasm was initially sparked off by my active participation in the debating society at school, of which I am president. I also follow the major legal cases in the newspapers and have visited the Old Bailey on a number of occasions.'

It is imperative that you make your personal statement relevant to the course of study that you wish to follow. This may sound like an obvious point but it is a common pitfall. The personal statement should state why you want to study law and what made you think of this as a degree course of study. Make sure that for each point you make, whether that be which A levels you are studying or the work experience that you have done, you are relating it back to the structure of the course or the modules of interest on the course. A sample personal statement is shown below.

My interest in law started after a school trip to the local magistrates' court, where we were allowed to do a mock trial. Before this, I had thought that the outcome of a trial was dependent only on the verbal skills of the defence or prosecuting lawyers: I had not realised how structured the process was, or how much control the judge has over proceedings. As a result of this, I joined the school's debating society, which has given me the confidence to present arguments in a structured and convincing way.

To gain more insight into a legal career, I arranged work-shadowing with a local law firm for two weeks. Whilst confidentiality issues prevented me from being able to actively get involved, I was able to see how much paperwork was involved, and the importance of accuracy in the work they did. I was able to help with some of the work that they were doing, including conveyancing and planning issues.

I chose my A level subjects with a law degree in mind. Economics and history both require analytical skills, the ability to draw conclusions from documents, and to be able to argue the case for these conclusions. I enjoy the way that events can be interpreted in many different ways, and the need for careful assessment of 'evidence'. The recent global economic problems illustrate that even experts do not always get things right. French has been very useful, because it not only requires a good memory and the ability to learn material; but also because I have chosen to do my A2 coursework on the French legal system and how it differs from our system. I hope that I can work for an international law firm in the future, and so this research will be useful. At AS level I also studied art. Whilst this is not directly relevant to law, I believe that using my creative skills to take ideas and turn them into something new and exciting is a useful ability to have; and I also enjoy art very much.

I keep up to date with current political and legal issues by reading broadsheet newspapers and using the BBC website. I have recently read 'Memoirs of a Radical Lawyer' by Michael Mansfield, which showed me that lawyers can have an effect on highlighting political as well as legal injustices.

As you will by now realise, it is not necessary to study law at university in order to become a lawyer (although it saves you a year of study). Here is a sample personal statement for a non-law course.

Since studying Shakespeare's tragedy of the star-crossed lovers, 'Romeo and Juliet', for GCSE, the underlying philosophical themes and references within English literature have intrigued me. My fascination stems from the multiple possibilities of meanings within a book, play or poem and the impossibility of there being a right or a wrong answer to a philosophical problem. I am excited at the prospect of studying literature combined with philosophy and see it as a way of broadening my mind and approach.

I have enjoyed studying a variety of different genres of literature and been enthralled by the questions raised and, subsequently, their answers. I have particularly enjoyed studying 'Hamlet', and found that to understand Hamlet, one must share the character's ability to philosophise and thus increase one's understanding of 'the question'. John Milton also presents a philosopher in his protagonist in 'Samson Agonistes'. Samson philosophises throughout the poem, striving to decide on a course of action. Eventually, his 'suicide' proves to be a moral triumph whilst fulfilling God's purpose. Jean-Paul Sartre's 'In Camera' is particularly interesting. The protagonists Inez and Estelle explore both Plato's cave theory and Immanuel Kant's theory of the veil of perception. Many philosophies have been constructed surrounding Mary Shelley's 'Frankenstein'. The wretch could simply be a monster or perhaps the fallen angel. However, Ursula Le Guin used Jung's theory of the shadow to suggest that the wretch is a projection of Frankenstein's evil half. In contrast, Rousseau suggests that the monster 'was born benevolent and good' but was corrupted by the society in which he was born. Similarly, when studying art, one only needs to look at art from the Renaissance to see the 'rebirth' and increased importance of philosophy. Raphael illustrates this in his 'School of Athens' where he portrays philosophers amongst 'Renaissance men', saints and his patrons.

The rest of the page should tell the admissions tutor all about what makes you who you are. For example:

- what travel have you undertaken?
- what do you read?
- what sporting achievements do you have?
- what music do you like or play?
- what responsibilities have you been given?
- what prizes or other awards have you achieved?

In all these areas give detail.

> Last year I went to Paris and visited all the Impressionist galleries there. I relax by reading American short stories – Andre Dubus and Raymond Carver amongst others. My musical taste is largely focused on opera (I have seen 14 productions of 'The Magic Flute') and I would like to continue playing the cello in an orchestra at university. I would also enjoy the chance to play in a football team to keep myself fit.

This is much more impressive than saying:

> Last year I went to France. I like reading and listening to music and sometimes I play football at weekends.

General tips: caution!

- Do not attempt to copy passages from other sources and incorporate them in your personal statement. UCAS uses anti-plagiarism software when checking statements: if you have used material from someone else (including the examples in this book), you will be caught out and your application will be void.
- Don't be tempted to get someone else (a friend, teacher, parent or one of the many internet sites that offer 'help') to write your personal statement. It has to sound like you, which is why it is called a **personal** statement.
- Although you can apply for up to five institutions or courses, you only write one personal statement, and so it needs to be relevant to all of the courses you are applying for. You will not be able to write a convincing statement if you are applying to a variety of different courses (see below).
- Print off a copy of your personal statement so that you can remind yourself of all the wonderful things you said, should you be called for interview!

- If you are planning to do so, state your reasons for applying for deferred entry and outline what you intend to do during your gap year. For example, you might be planning to find some relevant work experience in a firm of solicitors, and then spend some time overseas to brush up your language skills.

Warning: mixing courses and Joint Honours courses

As stated above, you write one personal statement which is read by admissions staff at the five courses for which you are applying. Each university only sees its name and course code on the form that UCAS sends to it: your other choices are not revealed. So, if you are applying to read psychology at one university (remember, you do not have to read law at university to become a lawyer), management at another, history at a third, and so on, then you cannot possibly write a personal statement that will satisfy the criteria for each of the courses. The psychology selector will wonder why you have written about history, and so on. The likelihood is that you will be rejected by all of your choices.

Similarly, if you apply for a Joint Honours course such as economics and history, your form will be seen by selectors from both departments, each of whom will want to see that are a serious candidate for his/her course.

Many universities offer very detailed advice about what they are looking for in a personal statement; and some will reject you if your statement does not conform to what they are looking for. Even if you are not going to apply there, the London School of Economics website contains some very useful advice on writing personal statements (www.lse.ac.uk).

Tips from admissions tutors

- Apply early
- Check for spelling and grammatical errors
- Focus your personal statement on the course you are applying for
- Make your personal statement sound like you
- Get work experience if possible
- Keep up to date on current issues.

The LNAT

The LNAT is the National Admissions Test for Law. It is an externally set test which is used by a number of universities to assist them in selecting suitable candidates either for interview or for conditional offers. Each university will use the LNAT result in a different way. Some may set a threshold mark which must be reached in order for a candidate to be considered, whilst others may use the LNAT result as just one of a number of factors that they will look at in assessing a candidate. There is no 'pass mark' for the LNAT. Further details of how each university uses the LNAT result can be found on their websites.

- To sit the LNAT, you must register on the LNAT website. The test is sat at an external test centre.
- The cost of the test (for 2012 entry) is £50 at UK and EU test centres, and £70 for other centres. The fee is payable online by credit or debit card.
- You can only sit the test once in any application cycle. If you sit it a second time, the later result will not count.
- If you reapply to universities that require the LNAT in subsequent years, you will have to sit the LNAT again.
- Information for candidates who may need extra time (for example, students with dyslexia) or need special arrangements (for example, students with sight or mobility problems) can be found on the LNAT website (www.lnat.ac.uk).

The LNAT is used by the following universities:

- Birmingham
- Bristol
- Durham
- Glasgow
- King's College London
- Nottingham
- Oxford
- University College London.

The deadline for sitting the LNAT is normally 20 January (1 November for Oxford), but check the LNAT website (www.lnat.ac.uk) for details.

The test lasts two-and-a-quarter hours and has two sections – a multiple choice paper and an essay.

The multiple choice paper (95 minutes) consists of 42 questions, based on passages. The questions do not require any legal knowledge, but are aimed to test candidates' powers of comprehension, deduction and analysis. The score for this section is sent directly to the university or universities.

The essay section (40 minutes) tests the candidate's ability to construct logical, structured and clear arguments. The essay is not marked by LNAT but is passed on to the universities.

Details and specimen questions can be found on the LNAT website.

For more help on the LNAT admissions tests read *Practise & Pass Professional: LNAT* (Trotman, 2011).

Cambridge University

Cambridge University stopped using the LNAT test in 2010. It has replaced it with the Cambridge Law Test, a one-hour paper that is normally sat when you attend your interview. Details can be found on the Cambridge University website (www.law.cam.ac.uk).

8 | Succeeding at interview

Outside Oxford and Cambridge, formal interviews are rarely part of the admissions process. Even at highly respected institutions such as King's College London and University College London, interviews are not the norm for all candidates and are usually reserved for those from a non-traditional background and some mature candidates. They are expensive and time-consuming for both the university and the applicants. However, although academic interviews are rare, they do occur, so if you're invited to attend one, here are some points to bear in mind.

Oxbridge examples

Sample interview questions, and even video examples are available on the websites of Oxford and Cambridge University. See the following websites:

- www.ox.ac.uk/admissions/undergraduate_courses/how_to_apply/interviews/index.html
- www.ox.ac.uk/admissions/undergraduate_courses/finding_out_more/podcasts/tenth_episode_the.html
- www.cam.ac.uk/admissions/undergraduate/interviews

Remember that if you shine in your interview and impress the admissions staff, they may drop their grades slightly and make you a lower offer.

What you need to know

Interviews need not be as daunting as you fear. They are designed to help those asking the questions to find out as much about you as they can. It is important to have good eye-contact and confident body language and view it as a chance to put yourself across well rather than as an obstacle course designed to catch you out.

Interviewers are more interested in what you know than in what you do not. If you are asked a question you don't know the answer to, say so. To waffle simply wastes time and lets you down. To lie, of course, is even worse – especially for aspiring lawyers!

Remember that your future tutor might be among the people interviewing you. Enthusiasm and a strong commitment to your subject and, above all, a willingness to learn, are extremely important attitudes to convey.

An ability to think on your feet is vital . . . another prerequisite for a good lawyer. Pre-learned answers never work. Putting forward an answer, using examples and factual knowledge to reinforce your points, will impress interviewers far more. It is also sensible to admit defeat if your argument is demolished.

It is possible to steer the interview yourself to some extent. If you are asked something you know nothing about, confidently replacing that question with another related one yourself shows enthusiasm.

Essential preparation includes revision of the personal statement section of your UCAS application, so don't include anything on your form if you're unprepared to speak about it at interview.

Questions may well be asked on your extra-curricular activities. Most often, this is a tactic designed to put you at your ease and therefore your answers should be thorough and enthusiastic.

At the end of the interview, you'll probably be asked if there is anything you would like to ask your interviewer. If there is nothing, then say that your interview has covered all that you had thought of. It is sensible, though, to have one or two questions of a serious kind – to do with the course, the tuition and so on – up your sleeve. It is not wise, obviously, to ask them anything that you could and should have found out from the prospectus.

Above all, end on a positive note and remember to smile!

Preparation for a law interview

The advice below is based on the assumption that you will be taking a Single Honours law degree, but if you have chosen a Joint or Combined Honours course then obviously you will have to prepare yourself for questions on those subjects as well. The interview is a chance for you to demonstrate knowledge of, commitment to and enthusiasm for the law. The only way to do this is to be extremely well informed. Interviewers will want to know your reasons for wishing to study law and, possibly above all, they will be looking to see whether you have a mind capable of developing logical arguments and the ability to articulate such arguments powerfully and coherently.

Much of the practice of law in this country rests on an adversarial system, so don't be surprised if you receive an adversarial interview.

Remember to keep calm and think clearly!

Reasons for wishing to study law vary. A passion for courtroom drama, *The Bill* or *Law and Order* is not enough. You need to think about the everyday practice of the law in this country and it is extremely useful to spend time talking with lawyers of all kinds and learning from them what is involved.

It is important to be aware of the many types of law that lawyers practise – criminal, contract, family, taxation, etc. – and be clear about the differences between them. The essential differences between barristers and solicitors must also be clear in your mind.

Use of the media

As a serious A level candidate you should already be reading a 'quality' daily newspaper. *The Independent*, *The Times* and the *Guardian* all have law sections during the week. If you are really keen read *The Law Society Gazette* or *The Lawyer*, which are published weekly. Following detailed law reports in the press will give you further insight into the ways in which the law is practised.

Regular listening to the radio and watching television are vital. Much of the news has legal implications and these subjects are consistently discussed in the broadcast media. TV's *Question Time*, *Newsnight* and certain *Panorama*-style documentaries and radio's *Today* programme, *The World This Weekend* and *Today in Parliament* are all examples of potentially very useful programmes to help you build up a thorough knowledge of current events. Also regularly visit the legal websites mentioned in the 'Further information' chapter at the back of the book.

Knowledge of the structure of the legal and judicial systems is vital. You should know who the Lord Chief Justice is, who the Director of Public Prosecutions is and what he or she does. You should be aware of recent controversial legal decisions, who took them and what their consequences are or could be. Who is the Home Secretary and why is he or she important? What do you think should be happening in the prison system at the moment? What reforms would you like to see implemented in the running of the police force?

The format of the interview

Interviewers will ask questions with a view to being in a position to form an opinion about the quality of your thought and your ability to argue a particular case. You may be presented with a real or supposed set of circumstances and then be asked to comment on the legal implications of them. Is euthanasia wrong? What is the purpose of prison?

Recent events are very likely to form a large part of the interview. Ethical issues, political issues, police issues, prison reform issues – all of these are possible as the basis for questions at interview. An ability to see the opposite point of view while maintaining your own will mark you out as strong law degree material.

Don't forget that interview skills are greatly improved by practise. Chat through the issues mentioned above with your friends and then arrange for a teacher, careers officer or family friend to give you a mock interview.

The interview for work experience

Most of the above-mentioned tips would equally apply if you are going for an interview for work experience to a firm of solicitors or a set of chambers. However, in addition you should do the following.

- Research the firm/chambers thoroughly before interview. Look at their brochure and website.
- Plan in advance what you think your key selling points are to the employer and make sure you find an opportunity in the interview to get your points across.
- Prepare a few questions about the firm to ask your interviewer at the end. You can demonstrate your preparation here by asking them about something you have read about the firm/chambers recently, if appropriate.
- Dress smartly and appropriately. Lawyers tend to look quite formal.
- Remember a nice firm, confident handshake at the beginning and end of the interview.

Possible interview questions

Questions may be straightforward and specific, but they can range to the vague and border on the seemingly irrelevant. Be prepared for more than the blindingly obvious, 'Why do you want to study law?' question. But remember you wouldn't have been invited for interview unless you were a serious candidate for a place so be confident and let your talents shine through! Here are a few sample questions.

1. Have you spoken to any lawyers about their work? Have you visited any courts?
2. What makes a good judge/barrister/solicitor?
3. What area of law are you interested in?
4. What is the difference between the law of contract and the law of tort?
5. Have you read about any cases recently?
6. Should cannabis/euthanasia be legalised?

7. What are the pros and cons of fusing the two branches of the legal profession?
8. Should the police in this country be armed?
9. If you were in a position of power, would you change the current civil legal aid situation?
10. Should the police spend their time enforcing the laws concerned with begging?
11. What do you think of the recent law reforms?
12. What are your views on the handling of the Stephen Lawrence case?
13. Should Britain or any other country be intervening in situations like those in Afghanistan or Iraq?
14. What are your views on the right to silence?
15. How can you quantify compensation for victims of crime?
16. Should criminals be allowed to sell their stories as 'exclusives'?
17. Is it 'barbaric' to cane someone for vandalising cars?
18. How does the law affect your daily life?
19. What would happen if there were no law?
20. Is it really necessary for the law to be entrenched in archaic tradition, ritual and jargon?
21. How are law and morality related?
22. Do you believe that all people have equal access to justice?
23. What is justice?
24. Why do we send criminals to prison? What are the alternatives?
25. Should the media be more careful with the way in which they report real crime?
26. Is law the best way to handle situations such as domestic violence/child abuse/rape?
27. Should British law encompass the laws of ethnic minorities since this society is so multi-cultural?
28. What causes crime rates to increase?
29. Should trial by jury be more or less common?
30. Do you think capital punishment should be reinstated?
31. Would the law in this country be any different if there were no royal family?
32. You are driving along a busy road with the window down when a swarm of bees flies into your car. You panic and lose control of the car, causing a huge pile-up. Are you legally responsible?
33. A blind person, travelling by train, gets out at his/her destination. Unfortunately the platform is shorter than the train, and the blind person falls on to the ground, sustaining several injuries. Who, if anyone, can compensate him/her?

Tips for the interview

- Read your personal statement carefully before the interview.
- Make sure you arrive early.

- Dress comfortably, but show that you are taking the interview seriously: wear smart, clean clothes.
- Make eye contact.
- Be willing to listen as well as talk, and don't be afraid to ask questions if you are unsure of what the interviewer wants.
- Be willing to consider new ideas, if your interview involves discussion of legal or other current issues.
- Be yourself.
- Be enthusiastic.

9 | Non-standard applications

Not everyone decides that they want to be a lawyer at an early age. Many successful lawyers are people who started out down a completely different career path. Equally, just because you come from a country outside the UK, does not mean you cannot become a successful lawyer in the UK. Law firms and chambers welcome applicants from a wide range of backgrounds, and often have diversity initiatives in place. This chapter offers an overview on non-standard applications, but please contact individual universities, the Law Society or the General Council of the Bar for more information.

Graduates with degrees other than law

As discussed in Chapter 4, graduates do not need to return to undergraduate study in order to qualify as a solicitor or a barrister. Instead, you would need to convert your degree into a law degree by taking the Graduate Diploma in Law (GDL), before moving on to the vocational stage of training. See Chapter 4 for more details.

Mature students

Mature students who do not have a first degree may need to follow a degree course before following the steps outlined in Chapter 4. The alternative, non-graduate, route is also described in Chapter 4.

International students

International students are less successful than UK students (not EU students) at gaining law places at UK universities, as the figures for 2010 entry show. This is, however, in contrast to the statistics in 2008 as international students have now overtaken EU students in all acceptances to law courses in the UK. Bear in mind though this is a marginal increase and the relevant statistic is the decrease in the number of acceptances to EU students last year.

Table 1: Nationality and success rate

Applicants' nationality	Number of applicants	Places	% Success
UK	20,323	18,008	89%
EU	1,922	1,215	63%
Non-EU	3,972	2,690	68%

The process of applying as an international student is similar to that used by UK students: you use the same online form, provide the same information, and have the same deadlines. The differences are likely to be these.

- The examinations you have taken and/or will be taking may not appear in the drop-down menus on the UCAS form.
- The fee codes and support arrangements will be different.
- Your school may not have registered with UCAS and so you have to apply as a private individual rather than through an institution.

Detailed advice about how to fill in the UCAS form, and to deal with these issues, can be found in the 'Students' and 'International Students' sections of the UCAS website (www.ucas.com).

However, many well-qualified, serious and motivated international students are unsuccessful in their applications because they or their referees (or both), are unfamiliar with what the university selectors are looking for. This applies to two sections of the application form:

1. the personal statement
2. the reference.

The personal statement

Students who have applied for universities outside of the UK may be familiar with the idea of writing a statement about themselves to support their applications. These can often take the form of a 'hard sell', in which the student extols his or her personal qualities, achievements, hopes and dreams. This format is not suitable for a UCAS personal statement, which needs to focus on the course itself, and what he or she has done to investigate it. The advice given in Chapter 7 is equally applicable to international students, and you should read it carefully.

The reference

Often, a promising application is rejected because the person providing the reference is unfamiliar with what is required, and the selectors have no choice other than to reject because they are not given enough information. UCAS references need to focus on the following:

● the student's suitability for the course and level of study
● an assessment of the student's academic performance to date (including the student's level of English if this is not his or her first language)
● how the student will adapt to studying in the UK
● the student's personal qualities.

If you are unsure as to whether the person who will write your reference fully understands what is required, show them the section on the UCAS website called 'Non-UK Advisors'.

LNAT

Some universities require candidates to sit the Law National Admissions Test (LNAT) in addition to gaining academic qualifications. This online test can be sat outside of the UK. See Chapter 7 for details.

Academic qualifications

The UCAS website (www.ucas.com) gives details of the acceptable non-UK qualifications. The international sections on individual university websites will provide further details. International students whose local qualifications are not acceptable to UK universities will need either to study A levels or the equivalent (at an international school in their own country) or at a school or college in the UK or follow a one-year university Foundation course. Details of providers of UK qualifications can be found on the British Council website (www.britishcouncil.org.uk).

10 | Results day

A level results day is arguably one of the most important days of your life, but don't panic: this chapter will provide you with some calm and practical advice on what to do on the day, whatever your results are.

The A level results will arrive at your school on the third Thursday in August. The universities will have received them a few days earlier. It is imperative that you go into school on the day the results are published. Do not wait for the results slip to be posted to you. Try to get hold of your results as soon as possible on the day, because if you need to act to secure your place or go through Clearing then time is of the essence because you will be competing with other students in the same situation.

Hopefully, you will need to do nothing other than celebrate! If you have a conditional offer and your grades equal or exceed that offer, then you can relax and wait for your chosen university to send you joining instructions. To check that all is in order, you can log on to the 'Track' facility on the UCAS website.

> **Tip!**
>
> One word of warning: you cannot assume that grades such as A*AB will satisfy an AAA offer. Always check with your chosen university.

If your results are not as good as you had expected, or better than you expected, or you did not receive an offer from any of your chosen universities, then there are a number of options.

What to do if your grades are significantly better than anticipated

UCAS has introduced a new scheme called Adjustment, which is aimed at applicants who achieved better grades than predicted. It is primarily designed for students who might have been predicted low grades and therefore applied to universities that would accept them rather than where they really wanted to go. The Adjustment system allows these students to hold on to their existing offers for a short period of time whilst contacting other universities where the standard offers are higher to see whether they will offer a place. Full details can be found on the UCAS website.

What to do if you have no offer

If all of the universities that you applied to rejected you, you are then eligible to enter a scheme called UCAS Extra. This allows you to apply to other universities, either for law or for other courses. You will automatically be sent details by UCAS. UCAS Extra starts in March. If UCAS Extra does not provide you with an offer, you can enter Clearing in August once you have your results – see more details on Clearing below.

If you did not receive any offers when you applied, perhaps because your AS results were not particularly strong, but you have ended up with better A level results than expected, then you need to make universities aware of this. The best way to do this is by email, and your UCAS referee may be able to help you in this respect. Try to persuade your referee to ring the admissions officers on your behalf – they will find it easier to get through than you will, or email a note in support of your application.

Having said all of this, it is a reality that due to the popularity of law as a degree, that you should not pin all of your hopes on obtaining an offer or place through UCAS Extra or Clearing. You may find that despite your best efforts, there simply are not any places available on law courses at universities where you would want to study. In which case, your best option would be to wait and reapply in the following academic year with your A level results to support your application. Given what has been said about the importance of choosing your university law course in Chapter 6, you do not want to settle for any university just because they have a place available, but hold out for a place at a better university and in the meantime build up your CV by getting some work experience.

What to do if you hold an offer but miss the grades

If you have only narrowly missed the required grades (either for your 'firm' or 'insurance' choice) it is important that you and your referee contact the university as soon as possible on results day, because you may be able to persuade the university to still accept you.

If you miss the grades for your firm choice, but meet the grades for your insurance choice, you will automatically be accepted onto the insurance place.

If you do not achieve the grades required for either your firm or insurance choice, and you are unable to persuade the university to still accept you, then you are eligible to enter Clearing. This is a list of places that are still available on various courses at all of the universities, and the list is published in national newspapers and the UCAS website. As mentioned above, places on law degrees available through Clearing will be few and far between, but if there is a place available at a university you would be interested in going to, then you must contact the university by telephone as quickly as possible on results day, because you will be competing with other students in the same position.

If you are unable to obtain a suitable place through Clearing, then you can either apply in the next academic year to courses for which you meet the entry requirements, or you may want to consider retaking some or all of your A levels.

Retaking your A levels

This may be a sensible option for students who know they are capable of achieving better grades than they did first time round. However, one thing to bear in mind is that the grade requirements for retake candidates are often higher than for first-timers. You should contact the universities to find out what they require from retake students. Many A levels can be retaken in January, but this depends on the board as well as the subject. The school or college where you will sit the retakes will be able to advise you in this respect.

Independent sixth-form colleges provide specialist advice and teaching for students considering A level retakes. Interviews to discuss this are free and carry no obligation to enrol on a course, so it is worth taking the time to talk to their staff before you embark on A level retakes.

Extenuating circumstances

If your grades were below those that were predicted or expected because of extenuating circumstances such as illness, family problems or other problems during the examination sitting, make sure that you have written confirmation of this (such as a letter from a doctor, solicitor or someone at your school or college) and fax or scan and email this to the admissions department for your chosen course.

Ideally, if something does go wrong at the time you are sitting your exams, you or the school/college should inform the universities immediately, warning them that you might not achieve the grades. It is more likely that they can make concessions then rather than when they have already made decisions about who to accept when the results are issued.

11 | Fees and funding

As you are most probably (and hopefully) aware, there have been significant changes to the fees and funding structure for universities, applicable from the 2012 academic year. These changes are due to the coalition government removing the subsidised funding for university courses, and therefore raising the cap on the fees universities are allowed to charge students. The following section briefly outlines the new fee structure for UK and international students, but more information can be found at http://studentfinance-yourfuture.direct.gov.uk.

UK students

From September 2012, public universities in England can charge UK and EU new full-time students up to £9,000 a year in tuition fees, and many universities will be charging the maximum amount. Private colleges and universities are not subject to the £9,000 maximum, so can potentially charge even more. You should check the websites of individual universities or use the UCAS course finder facility to find out how much a particular university is intending to charge.

English residents

English residents will pay up to £9,000 wherever they study in the UK. English students can get a government loan for tuition fees, which they will only begin to pay back when they are earning over £21,000 per annum. Maintenance loans and grants are also available to help cover the cost of living whilst at university. English students whose family income is less than £25,000 per year can also apply to the National Scholarship Programme (NSP). More information on the NSP is available at www.bis.gov.uk/assets/biscore/higher-education/docs/n/11-730-national-scholarship-programme-year-one.

Welsh residents

Welsh residents will also pay up to £9,000 wherever they study in the UK. The loan system is slightly different though, as Welsh students can apply for a loan of £3,645 from the Welsh government. There are grants available for the difference between the loan and the full fee.

Northern Ireland residents

Northern Ireland residents will pay up to £9,000 if they study in England, Wales or Scotland, but they will only pay £3,465 if they study in Northern Ireland.

Scottish residents

Scottish residents will not pay any tuition fees if they go to a Scottish university, but they will pay up to £9,000 if they study anywhere else in the UK.

EU students

EU residents will pay up to £9,000 if they study in England or Northern Ireland, but won't pay fees if they study in Scotland. If they are studying at a Welsh university they will receive the same help as Welsh students (see above).

Non-EU international students

The fees for non-EU residents do not have an upper limit and will depend on the course and the university. International students should contact individual universities for information on the fees they will be charging non-EU residents.

12| Further information

Useful addresses

Solicitors

Institute of Legal Executives
www.ilex.org.uk

Solicitors Regulation Authority
www.sra.org.uk

The Law Society
www.lawsociety.org.uk

The Law Society of Northern Ireland
www.lawsoc-ni.org

The Law Society of Scotland
www.lawscot.org.uk

Barristers

The General Council of the Bar
www.barcouncil.org.uk

The Education & Training Officer
www.legaleducation.org.uk

The Faculty of Advocates
www.advocates.org.uk

Inns of Court

Gray's Inn
www.graysinn.info

The Inner Temple
www.innertemple.org.uk

Lincoln's Inn
www.lincolnsinn.org.uk

The Middle Temple
www.middletemple.org.uk

General

Legal Action Group
www.lag.org.uk

Crown Prosecution Service
www.cps.gov.uk

Institute of Professional Legal Studies
www.qub.ac.uk/ipls

Useful books

There are a vast number of books written about the law and the legal profession and new ones are constantly being published. It is worth a trip to your school library, your local public library and your careers office to check what is available. Here are some we think might be useful to you.

The legal profession

Ivanhoe Career Guide to the Legal Profession, Richard Green, Cambridge Market Intelligence. (An overview of the legal profession)

GTI Law Journal, GTI. (Practical information about life as a solicitor or barrister, written by practitioners)

GET 2012: Law, Hobsons. (An overview of career options in law)

Careers Uncovered: Law, Margaret McAlpine, Trotman. (What it's really like working as a lawyer, and tips on training, work experience and job applications)

Career Opportunities in the International Legal Field, William Slomanson, The Law Society. (Opportunities for qualified lawyers and law graduates worldwide)

Solicitors' & Barristers' National Directory, The Law Society.

Chambers UK Guide and *Chambers UK Bar Guide*, Chambers & Partners Publishing. (Comprehensive directories of firms of solicitors and barristers' chambers)

The Legal 500, John Pritchard, Legalease. (A detailed account of the UK legal profession)

Solicitors' Regional Directory – Your Guide to Choosing a Solicitor, The Law Society. (A list of every firm in practice by region and town)

The Guide to Work Experience for Intending Lawyers, GTI. (Information on getting vacation placements and mini-pupillages)

The Bar Directory, FT Law & Tax. (Details of chambers and barristers)

Chambers, Pupillages & Awards Handbook, GTI. (Details of chambers in England and Wales offering pupillages)

Prospects Legal, Central Services Unit.

Working in Law, Charlie Phillips, Trotman. (A definitive guide to getting a career in law for both graduates and non-graduates)

General books on higher education

Choosing Your Degree Course and University, Brian Heap, Trotman.

Entrance Guide to Higher Education in Scotland, Committee of Scottish Higher Education Principals.

Getting into Oxford and Cambridge 2013 Entry, Jenny Blaiklock, Trotman.

Guide to Student Money 2011, Gwenda Thomas, Trotman.

HEAP 2013: University Degree Course Offers, Brian Heap, Trotman.

How to Complete Your UCAS Application 2013 Entry, Beryl Dixon, Trotman.

UCAS Guide to Getting Into University and College, UCAS.

Which Uni? Find the Best University for You, Karla Fitzhugh, Trotman.

General books on law

There are a number of good introductory texts on English law and the processes of learning the law. Among the ones we would recommend are:

The English Legal System, Jacqueline Martin, Hodder & Stoughton.

An Introduction to Law, 4th edition, P Harris, Butterworths.

Learning Legal Rules, 3rd edition, J A Holland and J S Webb, Blackstone Press.

Learning Legal Skills, S Lee and M Fox, Blackstone Press.

The New Penguin Guide to the Law, John Pritchard, Penguin.

Studying law

Practise & Pass Professional: LNAT, Georgina Petrova and Christopher M Reid, Trotman.

Passing the LNAT, R Hutton, G Hutton and F Sam, Learning Matters.

Letters to a Law Student, Nicholas J McBride, Pearson Education.

Miscarriages of justice and the legal system

Memoirs of a Radical Lawyer, Michael Mansfield, Bloomsbury.

Blind Justice, John Eddleston, ABC-CLIO.

The Law Machine, Marcel Berlins and Clare Dyer, Penguin.

More Rough Justice, P Hill and M Young, Penguin.

Presumed Guilty: British Legal System Exposed, Michael Mansfield, Heinemann.

Standing Accused, M McConville, *et al.*, Clarendon Press.

Report of the Royal Commission on Criminal Justice, Runciman Commission, HMSO.

Miscarriageo of Justice: A Review of Justice in Error, C Walker and K Starmer (eds), Blackstone Press.

Trial by jury

Jury Trial, J Baldwin and M McConville, Oxford University Press.

A Matter of Justice, M Zander, Oxford University Press.

Civil Legal Aid: Smith & Bailey on the Modern English Legal System, S H Bailey and M J Gunn, Sweet & Maxwell.

Achieving Civil Justice, R Smith (ed), Legal Action Group.

Tomorrow's Lawyers, P A Thomas (ed), Blackwell.

Professional journals

Commercial Lawyer (a monthly magazine)

The Economist

The Law Society Gazette (available from the Law Society)

The Lawyer (a weekly newspaper for solicitors and barristers, www. thelawyer.com)

Legal Action (bulletin of the Legal Action Group)

Legal Business (available from Legalease)

National press

The Times (Tuesday)

The Independent (Wednesday)

Useful legal websites

Note that addresses may change.

Legal publishers

Butterworths: www.lexisnexis.co.uk
Legalease: www.legalease.co.uk

General

www.infolaw.co.uk
www.online-law.co.uk
www.prospects.ac.uk
www.bbc.co.uk

Education/training

www.bpplawschool.com
www.barprofessionaltraining.org.uk
www.lawcabs.ac.uk
www.college-of-law.co.uk
www.pupillages.com

Careers

www.chambersandpartners.com
www.lawcareers.net
www.lcan.org.uk (Law Careers Advice Network)
www.simplylawjobs.com

Glossary

Administrative law
One of the core subjects needed for a qualifying law degree. It usually teams up with constitutional law. It looks at the legal position of the government, public and local authorities and others who wield some kind of power over broadly defined policy, such as town planning and public health.

Advocacy
This is the role of representing someone in court, arguing the case on their behalf. Barristers are the traditional 'advocates' in the English legal system, but solicitors can also conduct advocacy in all courts if they have obtained a certificate of advocacy.

Bar
The collective term for the barrister profession. Before commencing the vocational stage of training, budding barristers are 'called to the Bar'. The General Council of the Bar (commonly known as the Bar Council) is the representative body for barristers.

Bar Professional Training Course (BPTC)
The name of the one-year vocational course that anyone wishing to train as a barrister must take after completing a law degree (or non-law degree followed by the Graduate Diploma in Law – see below). For more information on the BPTC see Chapter 4.

Chambers
A building where a group of barristers work from. Barristers working from chambers will be self-employed, but they work from the same building to save on administrative costs. You could compare barristers working from chambers to students sharing houses at university; it is cheaper than each having a one-bedroom property. Once barristers have finished their pupillage they must obtain a 'tenancy in chambers'.

Black Letter law
This is a very traditional approach to the study of law, and mostly examines law found in the law reports and statute books.

Civil law
Unfortunately this has several meanings. It can refer to Roman law but it is more likely to mean either:

- private law, i.e. all law other than criminal, administrative, military and church law, or

- the system of law which grew from Roman law as opposed to the English system of common law.

Clinical legal education

This is the opportunity for you to get some hands-on experience with real-life cases without being able to go hideously wrong. Students, under supervision from qualified practitioners, give free legal advice to clients and usually see a case right through from beginning to end.

Common law

Again, this can mean one of two things.

- It can refer to the system of law that started about 1,000 years ago in Britain. Up to then, each locality had its own customs and practices for dealing with problems and misdemeanours. So, common law was an attempt to iron out inconsistencies between different areas (basically so that the men at the top could ensure their incomes and maintain their power) by applying one set of rules to similar circumstances.
- Alternatively, common law is a term for case law: that is law made by judges in decided cases, rather than laws enacted by Parliament.

Constitutional law

This is one of the core subjects needed for a qualifying law degree and is usually combined with Administrative law (see above). Constitutional law is the set of rules that control what the Crown, judiciary, Parliament and government do in relation to the country and all the individuals within it. But the constitution of the UK remains largely unwritten, unlike those of most other states, and comprises statutes.

Contract law (law of contract)

This is one of the core subjects needed for a qualifying law degree. There is an area of overlap between the laws of tort and contract. The same set of circumstances can even lead to tortious or contractual actions, so look up tort as well. Also, get used to this sort of far-fetched question: 'Adam has a TV which he promises to sell to Brian. Before he gets the TV though, Brian arranges to sell it to Chris for a tidy profit. But Adam changes his mind about the deal and sells it to David instead. When David receives the TV, it has been badly damaged in transit so he calls Adam to complain. Adam directs David to the small print at the bottom of the receipt that passes all responsibility onto the haulier, and so on . . . Who owns the TV and who should pay for the repairs?' Yes, this is the kind of thing that tutors dream up to antagonise their students. It is an example of the law covering contracts, i.e. legally binding agreements (written, verbal or even implied) between two or more parties coming about as a result of offer and acceptance, although there are several other criteria that must be fulfilled too.

Core subjects

Currently these are constitutional and administrative law; contract law; tort law; criminal law; equity and trusts; European Union law; and property/land law. They make up a qualifying law degree that will exempt you from the GDL course after you graduate.

Criminal law

One of the core subjects. Crime is so often sensationalised that criminal law needs little introduction but a lot of explanation, since the media continually obscure the legal points with hype. The law basically defines those acts that are seen to be public wrongs and are therefore punishable by the state. Most crimes are made up of two elements – the act itself (*actus reus*) and the thinking behind it (*mens rea*), both of which must be proved 'beyond reasonable doubt' in court to establish guilt.

Crown Prosecution Service (CPS)

Established in 1986, the CPS, headed by the Director of Public Prosecutions (DPP), is responsible for virtually all the criminal proceedings brought by the police in England and Wales, although the lawyers within the CPS don't always bring a case to court.

Delict (law of delict)

The Scottish name for tort.

Equity

Half of the double act equity and trusts and one of the core subjects. It is a (still developing) body of legal principles. It originated in the Middle Ages when, if you felt the common law was letting you down, you could petition the King's Chancellor for a fair appraisal of the situation. The Chancellor was keen to see justice done and wasn't too bothered about the rigidity of the law. Even now, equity prevails over the rules of law, but the system of equity is no longer as arbitrary as before. The main areas of equity cover trusts, property and remedies (e.g. injunctions). Look up the 'Anton Piller' order, a more recent example of equity at work.

European Union law

One of the core subjects. This area of law looks at the institutions of the European Union and how laws made by the EU impact on the English Legal System. For more information see Chapter 2.

Evidence

Remember that Tom Hanks film where the plot hinges on whether or not it's OK to use a crucial piece of evidence in court? Well, he lied in *The Bonfire of the Vanities*, and it was the law of evidence that he broke. This law covers the presentation of facts and proof in court. It is often associated with hearsay evidence that isn't always admissible, but also covers topics like confessions and the credibility of witnesses.

Exemption subjects
See core subjects.

Graduate Diploma in Law (GDL)
This is also known as the Common Professional Examination (CPE) and is the one-year course that non-law graduates must take to convert their non-law degree into a law degree by covering the seven core subjects in one year. Once the GDL is completed, a person is then able to move onto the vocational stage of training: either the LPC to become a solicitor, or the BPTC to become a barrister.

Jurisprudence
This is essentially the philosophy and theories of law. Jurisprudence units get right down to grass roots level and usually examine law from a number of angles, such as natural law, Marxism and the critical school.

Justis
This is a legal database (www.justis.com) giving you access to law-related information on computer. Two other similar databases are Lexis (www.lexisnexis.co.uk) and Lawtel (www.lawtel.com).

Land law (property law)
No points for guessing that this looks at who has rights (equitable and real) in different types of property and how these rights or responsibilities may be established or transferred. It covers subjects such as mortgages, trusts, landlords and tenants, leases, easements and covenants.

Law school
Simply refers to the law departments within universities. Not to be confused with College of Law where students study their LPC.

Lawtel
See Justis.

Lay jury
This is a panel of 12 non-legally qualified people who are selected at random to decide the verdict in criminal cases in the Crown Court.

Legal Practice Course (LPC)
The vocational one-year course after graduation (with a qualifying degree) and prior to the two-year training contract, designed for intending solicitors.

Lexis
See Justis.

Moot
This is a mock courtroom trial. Some universities have specially made rooms for that really authentic feel, and others even go so far as to include video cameras to record your performance. But on the whole, moots are organised as extra-curricular/optional activities to improve

your confidence and help develop your legal skills of presenting a clear, logical argument and questioning a witness.

Obligations (law of obligations)
This is just another name for the laws of tort and contract.

Personal statement
This is arguably the most important part of the UCAS application procedure. It is where you basically tell the universities why you want to study law at university and why you think you would be a suitable candidate for a law degree. For guidance on writing a personal statement see Chapter 7.

Private law
These are those bits of the law that are concerned with the relations between individuals that really have nothing to do with the state, but that doesn't stop the state intervening in certain circumstances of course. The areas are family law, property law and trusts, contract and tort.

Property law
See land law.

Public law
Sometimes this is the core course constitutional and administrative thinly disguised. Strictly speaking, public law also includes areas like tax law and criminal law, since they too are concerned with the relationship between the state and its individuals.

Pupillage
This is the final stage of training to become a barrister, and involves shadowing a qualified barrister, either for one year or for two six-month periods. For more detail see Chapter 3.

Statute
A general word for a law passed by Parliament.

Statute book
The list of all statutes that are currently in force.

Substantive law
Virtually all universities put most of the emphasis on substantive law at the undergraduate level. It is simply that huge part of the law that deals with duties and rights and everything else that does not fall into the category of practice and procedure.

Tort
Imagine it's a hot August day. You're gasping for a drink so you go into a café with your friend who buys you a bottle of beer. As you refill your glass you spot something a little suspicious and on closer inspection realise it's the decomposed remains of a snail! Do you:

1. drink the beer?
2. tell your friend to ask for a refund?
3. kick up a real furore and bring an action in tort against the manufac-
   turer for negligence in production causing you to suffer shock and
   an upset stomach?

If your name was Mrs Donoghue and the year was 1928 then you'd go
for option 3 and win the case, marking a milestone for the tort of negligence in English law. Tort is largely concerned with providing compensation for people who have been wronged and suffered personal injury or
damage to their property through negligence, defamation, nuisance,
intimidation, etc.

Training contract
The name given to the two years after an LPC when you train as a kind
of apprentice solicitor. In some cases, you can reduce the time spent by
completing work placements as part of an undergraduate degree, but
even then the training contract will last a minimum of one-and-a-half
years.

Trusts
See equity. Taking the simplistic approach, trusts arise when someone
transfers property to you but you can't use it. This is because the property is held on your behalf by trustees until you're 18 years old. The
property is entrusted to these trustees until you are able to choose to
dissolve the trust and look after – or spend – the property yourself.